This book is heartbreaking, eye-opening, and hard to put down. In this true story, Hayley Redman takes us into her world of a husband living and dying of ALS and her daily struggle as his main caregiver. Hayley's style allows us to see the love and humor that has been in her life as well as the pain and sorrow. I appreciated her deep insights into life, death, and how others respond to these experiences. I highly recommend this book.

~ Laurie Mueller, M. Ed, author of *The Ultimate Guide on What to Do When Someone You Love Dies*.

Reading Ms. Redman's exceptionally moving, unexpectedly funny account of struggle and loss makes one thing clear: you want someone like her beside you when grief sweeps over your own life. Someone to fiercely advise you that you should grieve exactly as you need to, without comparing or justifying yourself to others, someone to make bang-on, hilariously inappropriate observations that let you know you're still capable of laughing, someone to give you hope that after living through your current pain you may be able to connect even more deeply with the people and the world around you. This beautiful book makes a compelling argument for opening up to love even when staring down the certainty of death.

~ Dr. Shannon Gifford, Clinical Psychologist, Breakwater Institute

Amateur Widow

HAYLEY REDMAN

The recollections in this book are my own.
If you remember something differently,
you should write a book.
~Hayley

Amateur Widow

Published by Hayley Redman Publishing

Copyright © 2023 by Hayley Redman

ISBN- 978-1-7389669-0-5 (print)
ISBN-978-1-7389669-1-2 (ebook)

www.hayleyredman.com

All rights reserved. No part of this publication may be reproduced, stored in a retrieval system, or transmitted, in any form or by any means; electronic, mechanical, photocopying, recording, or otherwise, without prior written permission of the publisher.

First printing July 2023

Printed in the United States of America

10 9 8 7 6 5 4 3 2 1

*To my sons, Donovan-Rhys and Dylan—
you are the best of me. This book is for you.*

ACKNOWLEDGMENTS

To all the people mentioned, without you there would be no book. Thank you.

To my editor, Joanne Moyle, who has been patient with my profanities, curbed my profanities, and drank wine because of my profanities. Thank you.

To Heather, who, after laughing and sharing past life stories together, absent-mindedly asked, "Oh my God! When is the book coming out?" Here it is. Thank you, my beautiful friend.

Contents

Acknowledgments vii

Chapter 1 Death Day 1
Chapter 2 Welcome to Canada 10
Chapter 3 Instructions for Saying Goodbye 20
Chapter 4 Diagnosis 22
Chapter 5 Death Notification—Level: Expert 32
Chapter 6 Take the Pill, Woman 41
Chapter 7 Cremation Socks 52
Chapter 8 The Devil Loves Desperation 60
Chapter 9 Grief Pie 71
Chapter 10 I "Sister" You 78
Chapter 11 The Funeral 90

The Greatest Dad who had ALS 95

Chapter 12 We All Fall Down 102
Chapter 13 Ashes to Eyelashes 112
Chapter 14 Happy Anniversary 120

Chapter 15 Taxes   129
Chapter 16 The Poisoning   142
Chapter 17 Scruff   161
Chapter 18 Right Down the (Feeding) Tube   170
Chapter 19 Fight Like a Girl   178
Chapter 20 Best-Laid Plans   191
Chapter 21 The First of Everything   201
Chapter 22 Fuck the Toronto Maple Leafs   212

About the author   218
Accolades and Praise for *Amateur Widow* . . .   219

CHAPTER 1

Death Day

I WAKE TO AN UNFAMILIAR SILENCE. Lying on the sofa, I focus on the absence of noise.

Wait, let me listen harder . . .

Oh my God—why is it so quiet? If I lie here and listen long enough, surely I will hear that familiar, congested, shallow breathing that assures me we have another day.

Nothing . . .

My mouth dries. I am too afraid to move. I hold my breath to complete the silence. My husband might be dead.

Death planning, in some form or another, had been occurring in my home for many years. The subject was broached, primarily by me. Most times, my husband would brush off the "nonsense talk" and end attempts at conversation about end-of-life planning. "None of that will matter when I'm better," was his typical comeback. I get it: What young father and husband wants to prepare himself to leave this world? Still, the fear of not knowing what to do when he was gone—or worse, getting it wrong—drove me to press him. I was afraid of carrying the burden of goodbye and I knew I should prepare my children and myself. I would be informed and organized for when the time came.

We would be ready.

For the terminally ill there exists an opportunity to brace for the inevitable tidal wave on the horizon. In our case, the water had been rising slowly for years—so imperceptibly that I didn't notice I had to live life on my very tiptoes just to breathe. The thing is, when that tsunami finally hits, it doesn't matter how many books you have read or how strong your shelter is; that water rises higher than you ever imagined.

My husband was dead. He looked peaceful. One of my in-laws quietly played Donovan's favorite music in the background. I held his hand and the family gathered for the anticipated goodbyes. We stood in silence, arm in arm, in support of one another while we watched the staff from the funeral home gently gather up his body and ceremoniously wheel the stretcher out. It was as if I were observing, outside of myself, as they gently placed him on top, bundled so neatly and securely as he left his home for the last time.

Except that none of this happened.

Death is a fucking mess ...

I was still holding my breath, trying to be silent enough to hear Donovan breathe. His congested rattle was so easily audible even without silence—but it was nonexistent. *Exhale, dammit!* Realizing that I couldn't stay immobilized, holding my breath all day, I pushed myself up and sat on the edge of my futon. I looked over at his still silhouette; his chest did not rise or fall. The dog and cat were not in their regular spots; one curled up in the crook of an arm, one between his legs. *Shit! Shit. Is this it? God, don't let it be today. It's today, I just know it . . .*

I found the courage to walk over to my husband and forced myself to stand, then take small, shuffled steps in his direction. I did not look up until I felt the metal of the hospital bed rail against my arm. It felt colder and more clinical than ever before. I raised my eyes to focus on Donovan.

He was gone.

I had wondered if I would be able to tell if he was dead or sleeping—but it was clear. He appeared to be made of wax, his dry, peeling lips just a shade darker than his pallid face. No, I could not wake him. I touched the arm outside of the covers to find that the warmth of my husband had been replaced with an alarming chill. I reached under the covers and laid a hand on his belly—he was cool there too. I doubled over to cry but no sound came out. Moving out of this makeshift hospital room, I met my baby sister, Kate, in the kitchen. I told her that I couldn't wake him. She then became "the big sister" as I asked her to rouse him. She couldn't; she knew this. I knew as well and yet, in some odd refusal to accept what had happened, I demanded that she try. I wanted her to reveal the healing power she had been hiding from me all these years, and wake him. I heard the irrationality arising from me as I begged for this to be undone. The weight of my despair pressed down on my sister as I forced her to tell me that he was gone, and no one could wake him.

My jet-lagged cousin Jonathan made his way toward Donovan. Having flown in from Heathrow, he had been in the country for less than twenty-four hours. I intercepted and stood in his way, holding up my hand—a stop sign—as an attempt to save him from the pain, but he already knew. It was the very reason he'd made the journey from Wales—to be here for this juncture. Jonathan and Kate held me tight. We supported each other in those initial moments we knew were coming but were now, somehow, so unexpected. My mum magically appeared at the back door, and before I could make words come out, she said, "I know, my love." She assumed her role as caretaker of all and paused her pain to soothe mine. Instructions were provided and practical plans were made that brought calm to the chaos I had created.

Good thing I was prepared for this.

Does one ever think about what should be done when one's husband is found dead? Granted, it is likely a little less alarming when the death was preceded by a terminal illness. But the truth is, I was shocked at my shock. I had known for quite some time that my husband would die, but

I had never considered that I would see his dead body. In my version of preparation, there was the struggle of easing my love into the arms of death, followed by dreadful sorrow. His body would magically cease to exist at the exact moment he did, wouldn't it? And yet, there I was, sitting with a forsaken vessel, an unoccupied version of my former strong, spirited husband. And the love? It remained unwavering. How was it not enough?

Before the morning no longer belonged to us, we took what we needed from it. Some time. Some privacy. Kate brought water and some washcloths to Donovan's bedside. Mum checked the temperature with the back of her wrist before they gently washed him, brushed his hair, then lay him down, flat. For the first time in a very long time, he could lie down. No pressure on his bottom, no positioning based on optimal breathing. I closed my eyes for a second and remembered the last time we lay down together. They disconnected the things that tried in vain to keep him alive and made him presentable. Then he was ready for his audience.

I picked up the phone to make the first of many calls that had to be made, but this was the only call I had to do on my own. This one, from Canada to Wales, opened the floodgates of international sadness. This call, so very important to me, was the one where words refused to cooperate. It took me three attempts to get the sixteen-digit international phone number right and I said a silent thank-you for the extinction of rotary dials. It was picked up on the second ring with a cheerful "Hello?"

"I need Dad," was the greeting I gave to my father's girlfriend. She immediately understood what was coming and called him over. When he picked up the receiver, I managed to squeak out a weak "Dad," to which he replied and kept repeating, "Oh no. NO! No-no-no," until someone more responsible on each end took the handsets from us. On my father's end, I imagined his girlfriend, Sian, already finding flights and preparing to send my dad to me. On my end, my mum confirmed the news and hung up. How many times would I need to compose myself to function? How many times?

Jonathan made tea and we drank it beside Donovan's bedside. No one questioned it; we all instinctively went to sit with him. Just a group of tea drinkers and the recently departed—no biscuits though. That would be weird.

More phone calls were made, then tearful family and close friends filtered in. Our family doctor attended and sat with her stethoscope pressed to his chest and listened to the silence before formally pronouncing death. She cried with us. The funeral home staff arrived to collect his body but I was not ready to let him go. I sat with my husband and held his hand even though I knew that he was no longer there. I needed to remain with the body that betrayed us both because that was what I had left. After a while, my mum sat with me and then told me that it was time to go and shower.

"Do I smell?"

"No, you silly bugger," and we tried to smile. What she meant was that it was time to let him go. To decide that this was the last time I would ever see him or be near him. When I walked away from this room, my marriage would be over, my husband would be gone, and the world as I knew it would be forever different. I pressed his cold hand to my mouth. The pain of that moment was immeasurable.

Not for the first time, and certainly not the last, I sobbed in the shower while scrubbing at the injustice of loss until my skin reddened, but still, it stayed with me, a permanent stain. When I came out, I felt an ache across my chest from shoulder to shoulder, like I was being scooped and emptied out. I felt panic—I wanted to undo this and have more time, just one more day. One more conversation. One more anything. How did I not write down every word Donovan ever spoke? Why did I not record his voice? Why didn't I have more patience, love, and understanding for him? He was now gone. Physically taken away. I walked into the kitchen just in time to see the end of the funeral home stretcher being bounced down the ramp from our deck. The "body collectors" had been forced to wait outside until I was ready. They awkwardly stared at their shoes and shuffled about with their hands shoved deep into their pockets but were quick to spring to action when given the nod. I'm sure they could ill-afford this delay. Just standing around while some novice widow acclimatized. *Get it together, death amateurs. We have bodies to collect!*

What do you suppose is the daily average number of bodies collected from a smallish town? Just how busy are they? Do they have to take each body immediately back to the funeral home, or can they pick up all the deceased people that happen to be en route and load them for efficiency, like a macabre reverse delivery system?

The room at the back of our little house, which overlooked our garden, used to be a playroom. In recent months it became a homemade hospital room complete with devices, lifts, and machines that ping. Then it became a death room. Then it became uninhabitable. The room was emptied of borrowed medical devices. Companies and charities were quick to come and reclaim their feeding pump, IV pole, and hospital bed. All collections were meticulously choreographed to be completed while I sobbed in the shower. No unnecessary upsets happening here today. The leftover bedding was piled on the floor with the pillow on top. A gold angel pin, a gift to watch over Donovan and give him strength, was still fastened to the corner of the case.

YOU HAD ONE JOB, ANGEL PIN!!

I pick up the pillow and press it to my face to breathe in the faintly medicinal mixture of Head & Shoulders shampoo, bar soap, and that sweet nighttime familiarity that was my husband. What if I forget this smell? This moment? What if I won't recall his voice or his face? I needed to preserve every drop. In an inexplicably bazaar instant, I started a small but important quest. "I need a giant Ziploc bag," I said as I marched to a closet, searching and demanding others to do the same. My poor family stared at one another with tissues dabbing their blotchy eyes as if to say, "Well, that descent into madness happened quicker than expected." But they did as they were told, because, when a new widow asks you to do something, you just do it. I found what I was looking for and triumphantly packaged the pillow, along with its precious smell and the angel of betrayal, into a vacuum bag and squeezed out all of the air. I had saved this "smell-memory" and would sparingly indulge whenever I needed to feel close to my husband.

The room transformed from a hospital room into just a room. Check.

Husband smell preserved forever. Check

Dead husband removed from home. Check

Up next: Get our boys from school and tell them that their daddy was dead.

CHAPTER 2

Welcome to Canada

I TOOK A GAP YEAR following sixth form college to travel and work as an au pair. (For those of you who aren't familiar, sixth form is the last two years of secondary school in Wales as well as England and Northern Ireland.) I had already been accepted to university and planned to become a teacher but thought I should stretch my legs a little before settling into more higher learning. As soon as exams were over, I packed a bag and took my pasty, freckly skin off to Ontario, Canada. I would be back in London to start a new nanny job in the autumn. My parents had lifelong friends that had moved to Canada from Wales years before, and they took me in and treated me like one of the family. When I was eleven, we visited Canada for the first time as a family. I discovered Timbits, got lost in Canada's Wonderland, and kissed an Orca at MarineLand in Niagara Falls. (No judgment please. I was eleven years old and oblivious to the atrocities of keeping marine animals in small tanks. My parents also lacked that social conscience; they had just stopped smoking in the car with my sister and me about two minutes ago, so animals held in captivity solely for entertainment purposes was a yet-to-be-exposed concern.) My sweet sweatshirt that said *I KISSED A WHALE* across the front was relegated to the darkest corners of my closet. Animal abuse aside, I fell in love with the mysterious land of Canada and the funny-talking people who called it home.

Soon after I arrived that summer, my adopted Welsh Canadian parents and I went to visit British friends of theirs in the same town. Their house was twenty minutes away and, as a slightly naïve Welshwoman, I found it shocking that one could drive twenty minutes and still be in the same town. It was early days, but on this trip I had only met other Brits. My guess is that this was due to a mass exodus in the seventies where everyone wanted a fresh start. But that fresh start would ideally be with the same people they were used to. That way, if they could go to the same sort of pub they were used to and re-create the same atmosphere thousands of kilometers away, all the better.

We were drinking tea (obviously) in the living room of these English folk when a rather grumpy, very sweaty, mysteriously sexy man came panting through the front door. There were no introductions or conversations. He didn't even glance my way. (Ummm, hello? Gorgeous redhead here. Are you blind?) I gathered that he was their son because his mother mentioned that his work lunch was ready "int-fridge," and his dad asked, "How was your run, Son?" in his broad Northern England accent.

On the drive home, my hosts filled in the blanks. Mystery grump was indeed the son. He had recently returned from serving his country in the Royal Canadian Navy and was newly divorced from a woman with whom he had lived—along with a daughter—in British Columbia. The ex-wife and daughter were still in BC so he was grumpy about all of that highly complex, adulting stuff. I immediately labeled him as old. Clearly, not someone worthy of further investigation or a little holiday fling. My "fling guy" would not have amassed such a sizable degree of grown-up problems. After all, I was an eighteen-year-old who still automatically assumed that her parents would pay the restaurant bill. These life problems were beyond my delicate years.

Why mention this grumpy individual if he were immediately put out of mind?

Yes, there is more...

The following weekend, all of the local British people went to a pub to socialize, play pool, and sing karaoke. The Grump was there and we were formally introduced. His name... Donovan, the same name as his father. He seemed a tad less grumpy, was a confident dancer, and challenged me to a game of pool. He had a huge smile and was evidently aware of his good looks. Surprisingly, getting a turn at singing karaoke was a challenge that required aggressively acquiring a pencil so you could add your name to the waitlist. I was coerced into a duet with Donovan and we sang the B52's "Love Shack," which of course sounded better than the original. I knew that I was a fabulous singer —ask anyone who's been in the car with me—but I was surprised at how well Donovan could carry a tune. Later in the evening, he sang solo. By that time, I had to close one eye to see straight, but my hearing was fine. He sang "The Dance" by Garth Brooks, and the entire place went silent. I was gobsmacked, jaw dropping, mouth gaping in awe.

"Blimey!" I turned to the person next to me. "Can you believe his voice?"

"Yeah, he's pretty well known for his karaoke Garth Brooks renditions," they answered. When he finished his song, I offered him some singing pointers so that next time he could really nail that performance. I had to shout my advice over the applause and demands for "MORE!" that filled the pub full of drunken fools.

Later the following week, he called the house landline (because there was no other option for communication). The announcement that he was on the line was bellowed through the house. I ran to the kitchen and reached over the table to pick up the receiver and stretched the curly cord as far as it would go so I could hide my glowing cheeks. Donovan asked if I would like to be "shown around town a bit." I did want that, even though it meant substantial teasing from the kitchen dinner crowd, causing those cheeks to burn rosier. No big deal—he was an adult with a past marriage and experience. I was a kid. What could possibly happen?

The "not-a-date" went well and I discovered that he was, in fact, very immature. I honestly had no idea how he stumbled into such huge adult responsibilities with clearly very limited emotional capacity. He didn't seem like any dad I knew. He took me to a number of his favorite places including a boxing gym that had an eye-watering smell of forgotten dirty laundry. I was close to writing him off for the unnecessary assault on my olfactory senses when I realized that he had brought me to that place to show off. He was like a celebrity; everyone knew him and stopped what they were doing to give him the appropriate man-hug or backslap. The walls had framed pictures of him boxing, training, and receiving medals. An old, weathered man who called Donovan "Champ" asked, "Who is this lucky girl?" I was introduced to his coach, who told me about Donovan's amateur boxing career and how he was once the Ontario champ in his age and weight class. This was 100 percent a showboating outing to impress me. The nerve! It totally worked. He was funny, smart, sexy, and that body! Suffice to say, he was definitely in the running for a summer fling. We did all of the regular date things and were soon seeing each other several times a week. When we weren't on a date, he would call to tell me that he was right about the plot twist on *L.A. Law* or why I should learn to love Garth Brooks and country music in general. Or that I had grown up in a third-world country because I had never seen an episode of *Seinfeld* and had never experienced poutine. He was going to rectify all of that. Mostly, I just wanted to get him naked.

But there was one date in particular that became the game changer. On cheap-night Tuesday, he took me to see the Whoopi Goldberg film *Sister Act*. It was a popular spot so we put our jackets on our seats before heading to the lobby for popcorn. When we returned, our belongings were on the floor in the aisle and our seats were occupied by one of two couples that had arrived together. I picked up our things and Britishly apologized before pointing out that we had left our jackets on the seats to reserve them. The man in the aisle seat did an exaggerated lean over the arm of the chair to be closer to my face and loudly replied, "Fuck off." I could feel his hot cigarette breath on my face. A quiet fell over the cinema as rude thug number one laughed with his friend at his quick wit and bravado. Had I been back home, those would have been fighting words. I would have attempted to rip that fucker out of his seat by his nasty hair and no one would have been allowed to stay for the film. However, being a foreigner, and on a date, I wasn't ready to reveal my feisty side.

"Let's find new seats." I gave in. Donovan calmly moved in front of me and asked the man if he could have a quick word. At the same time, he pulled him from his seat while rotating him into the wall behind us. There was no hitting and no raised voices as he leaned his chest against the other guy's and said something that I couldn't hear. Donovan then stepped back and gestured for the man to leave the space. I am pretty sure that thug number one quietly repeated his classic one-liner insult but did so as he hurried out of the cinema, leaving his friends and date behind. Donovan turned to the remaining group and asked if he could have a quick word with them. They gathered up their popcorn and smuggled-in beers along with their friend's abandoned snacks, saying they would find other seats. Donovan enthusiastically said, "Awesome! Thanks, guys! I appreciate it." He then motioned for me to take my seat and apologized to the couple behind us for the disturbance before he sat down. I was shaking and my mouth was dry. I couldn't tell if I was just terrified by the altercation or embarrassed by the unexpected insult. What I did know was that I had never been so attracted to someone in my life before that moment. I tried to focus on the film but already knew I would have to rent this masterpiece when it finally made it to video because most of my concentration was directed to not sliding off my seat.

That summer could not have been more perfect. I soaked up every second of dating an older man and traveled around North America. We drove to Chicago, Florida, and everywhere in between, and, with each return to Ontario I would pick up the phone and call Donovan, who answered with "Welcome back, my beautiful girl. I missed you." I refused to think about returning to Wales. Not in a denial sort of way, more of an "enjoy the moment while you're in it" sort of way. The return flight had been booked but, with summer stretched out ahead, it was filed away under "nope, not thinking about that now." This trip was not real life. This was partying my way through summer, while having a wild holiday romance with the sexiest man alive. I was going to enjoy every moment before going back to the cloud-bound UK and settling into work, then school. Everything was exactly the way I had imagined. The trip had gone as planned; leaving Donovan, this lifestyle, and Canada was going to be horribly difficult. The sign of an amazing vacation.

The holiday had ticked all of the boxes, except suntan, and that is only because I am a pasty ginger capable of getting a sunburn while wearing SPF 50 sunscreen. I imagined myself staring out of a rain-soaked library window in Sunderland University while reminiscing of that perfect summer. It was part of a carefully mapped life plan. Comprehensive school, sixth form college, summer of fuckery, university / au pair, teacher training, meet a future husband (who is also a teacher so we have the same holidays), teach, marry, birth my own humans.

There would be NO DEVIATION.

I had a Sunday evening flight booked and would be landing in Heathrow early Monday morning. The Friday evening prior was spent with all the wonderful people responsible for making my holiday perfect. We had a backyard barbecue and sat around the fire, swatting at mosquitoes. I introduced Donovan to Sinead O'Connor; he thought "Nothing Compares 2 U" was depressing. I pointed out that he should shut his mouth while talking about a woman who can speak directly to my soul. Besides, while the country song that he had just played did have a more cheerful melody, the lyrics alluded to the singer's wife cheating on him with his brother on the day his truck broke down. Our teasing and laugh-filled banter was periodically interrupted with a gaze that was held a little too long or a gentle caress across my cheek. I'd be forced to break the seriousness with a kiss or an arm punch. Dude, keep it together! Don't fuck things up with feelings; we've had so much fun.

"What am I going to do without you?"

"Probably sing karaoke and try and find some other cute redheads to hit on."

"Let's disappear and spend tomorrow night together. It's your last night. I want you all to myself."

"As long as you're not going to be a weirdo and have feelings and shit."

"Heaven forbid!" He told me to pack an overnight bag and I gasped and replied with a shocked, "Sir! I certainly hope you don't plan on looking at my boobies."

He stood abruptly, tipping his plastic lawn chair, and shouted, "Madam! I hope you don't plan on looking at *mine*."

Of course, we'd already seen each other's boobies.

Donovan picked me up in his 1986 Ford Escort hatchback. We drove toward Lake Ontario and pulled into the car park of the Ascot Motel, a rough-looking place with a beat-up sign. Some of the bulbs behind the letters of the sign were burned out. Currently, it read, AS T MO EL. Donovan ran into the lobby, and I watched as he signed a book while charming the lady behind the counter, who was smoking a cigarette. He returned to the car with a massive plastic key tag with the room number written on it—just in case it was dropped in public, so the finder would know which room to burglarize. I jiggled the key in the lock and had to give the door a shove with my hip to open it. The room was dated and basic, but clean. It smelled faintly of smoke and a lot like floral-scented, powdered carpet freshener. The kind that gets vacuumed up. Heavy curtains were covering the huge window; I pulled them back and was pleasantly surprised to see that the motel backed onto Lake Ontario. The view of the shoreline was breathtaking. Donovan and I sat on our little balcony and enjoyed the view before leaving to eat dinner at a small, quiet restaurant. Later, we walked back to our room, holding hands, along the crowded lakefront park. We had to drink in every moment we had. The moon was full and bright and hung low over the lake, meeting its wavy reflection in the water. We kissed our way into the room where Donovan fired up his ghetto blaster and pulled me toward him.

"Dance with me . . ."

John Michael Montgomery sang "I Love the Way You Love Me," and Donovan sang along, word for word. Go ahead, reader—sift through the Spotify archives for that one. I'll wait . . . Just keep that playing in the background while I tell you that Donovan was wiping my tears with his thumbs as he told me this: "I love you more than I ever thought possible. Don't go back. Stay here with me. Please, stay here and be with me."

This was NOT the plan.

Two months after my nineteenth birthday, less than a year later, we were married. There would indeed be a deviation from the plan. Actually, there would be a deviation from *all the plans*.

CHAPTER 3

Instructions for Saying Goodbye

How to say goodbye to the nearly or dearly departed.

Attend in person, leave prior to death. My stepdaughter, Kylee, did this. She flew in from British Columbia. She and her dad were very close, and she wanted to see him. However, she did not want to see him die. This is the right way to say goodbye.

Attend in person, stay until post-death. My cousin Jonathan did this. He flew from Wales. He and Donovan were very close, and he wanted to stay for that part. This is the right way to say goodbye.

Attend in person, post-death. My dad did this. He flew to Canada from Wales. He and Donovan were very close, and he wanted his last memory to be of a different time. This is the right way to say goodbye.

Do both. If you live nearby, visit as much as you can, invest as much as is emotionally safe. This is the right way to say goodbye.

None of the above. Death is not for you. Remember in a way that meets your needs. This is the right way to say goodbye.

CHAPTER 4

Diagnosis

DONOVAN JOGGED THE LAST FEW STEPS of his run and came into the house. He was wearing an old Pepe sweatshirt with the armholes cut out so wide his latissimus muscles were visible. He leaned against the fridge, breathing heavy and guzzling water. His black hair stuck to his sweaty skin.

"You're cutting it fine," I pointed out. He planted a sweaty kiss on my cheek and assured me that he would be ready; his doctor always ran late anyway. I was annoyed because that wasn't the point. Or maybe I was worried and it made me irritable. Donovan's doctor had asked for us both to come in for his appointment.

Many months earlier, Donovan came home from the gym complaining that he felt weaker on one side. Specifically, when he was bench-pressing. One side was letting him down and preventing him from reaching that next goal. He paid attention to working the weaker side, hoping to build up strength. It didn't work. He had no pain but felt that the deficit was significant, so he made an appointment with our (useless, but the *whole* family used him so we blindly followed) physician. Donovan had measured the strength on both sides while lifting weights and explained his scientific findings to his doctor; he could lift about a cajillion pounds on one side but slightly less than a cajillion on the other, and no amount of effort equaled them out. The doctor smiled and pointed out that Donovan's weaker side was stronger than two of most men's sides put together. He placated him with an X-ray that revealed nothing and told him to keep an eye on it.

Weeks later, my frustrated husband stood in his underwear in front of our bedroom mirror and asked me if I could see it.

"See what? Your sexy, naked body?" I said, and ran my free hand across his abs. The heavy, damp baby on my hip grabbed a fist full of his chest hair. "See? We both want a piece of you." He winced and tickled his boy, making him extend those chunky legs and squeal with delight.

"No, seriously. When you look at me straight on, you can see that my right side is smaller. How does that make sense for a right-handed person who tries to work out the right side harder than the left?" I was stumped and, of course, he was right. As he stood facing the mirror, athletic and strong with his naturally olive skin tight over his lean body, his bulging shoulder muscles were indeed a little less bulgy on the right side.

Donovan went back to the family doctor, and over the months to follow there was another X-ray, followed by physiotherapy, cortisone injections, and massage. Nothing could explain the deficit between the two sides, and nothing helped resolve it.

We were sitting on the sofa one Sunday evening, watching the action classic *Twister* when Donovan asked me to roll up his T-shirt sleeve and look at his arm. A cow flew across a road in the grips of a tornado as I pressed PAUSE on the VHS tape. He had a twitch. I could see the skin move as the muscle rhythmically pulsed beneath it. He described it as annoying, coming and going for hours at a time over the past few days. It looked like a tiny foot, kicking to get out of his bicep. I made light of it by suggesting that this could be a tiny cow or possibly a tiny tornado, trapped in his arm. It was going to burst out, through his skin in the night, and we would be forced to take cover. Or, my more serious thought was maybe the muscle was a little excitable after hitting the gym pretty hard this week. He shrugged and agreed with my expert medical opinion, although I sensed skepticism.

The following Friday evening, after our baby, Donovan-Rhys, was in bed, we were about to sit on the sofa with a drink and snacks to watch the totally amazing drama *Primal Fear*. Donovan was fetching a beer for him and a cider for me while I rewound the tape that some rude, irresponsible renter had returned to Blockbuster Video before us. On the way back from the kitchen, the beer bottle slipped from his grip and bounced across the parquet floor, spilling foam as it gathered momentum. I jumped up to clean it up, pointing out the obvious and the oh-so-lucky lack of breakage. My husband stared at the hand that betrayed him and

I shrugged off the mishap as a coincidence because people drop things all the time. Especially me. I am the clumsiest of all! Acknowledged, we both dismissed the accident and neither of us admitted that a knot had developed in our respective stomachs. This uneasy, nagging suspicion clouded our casual dismissal of something we had labeled an accident. We knew that we would revisit this. Possibly, but not immediately, life was about to get distracting.

We had just signed the paperwork on the purchase of our first home. It was a tiny, turn-of-the-century bungalow that was in desperate need of TLC. It had room for our family to grow, a huge backyard, and it was ours. Well, technically, the bank owned it. We just lived in it, or we would, in the near future, once the portable propane heater had been removed and a proper furnace was installed. We spent a month cleaning a hundred years of cigarette smoke buildup and removing carpets made of toxic dust. Packing and organizing to move took priority over most things. Donovan-Rhys was scared of the sound of packing tape being pulled off the roll, so I left all of the boxes open until past the baby's bedtime. This would have been a great plan, except Donovan-Rhys would spend his waking hours tittering his wibbly body from box to box, unpacking and throwing his findings away once they were sufficiently covered in dribble. This did add some clutter and annoyed my husband, but Donovan-Rhys and I thought it was a winning strategy. The happiness and excitement of finally not renting and owning a home overshadowed Donovan's complaint of shoulder weakness, and mention of it diminished. That was until Donovan-Rhys unpacked a whole box marked MISC in permanent marker for the second time. A frustrated Donovan removed his son from the overturned box by pulling his ankles and sliding him out on his belly; he emerged, complete with a wooden spoon and a Tupperware triumphantly grasped, one in each fist.

"Take the destructor." He passed me a wooden spoon–wielding baby. "I'll tape these up so we can actually make some progress here." He took over the box-taping job, except his thumb and finger wouldn't cooperate; they wouldn't adequately grip. It felt as though he were pinching as hard as he could, and yet, the tape could not be pulled from the roll. He threw the roll of tape down, and as he left the room, snapped, "And I still have that damn arm twitch."

We moved into our new home three weeks before the doctor diagnosed a trapped nerve in Donovan's right shoulder and prescribed ultrasound therapy and more tests. One of the tests included stickers and wires over his body that measure the electrical impulses of muscles to better locate the offending nerve. This test was inconclusive but led to the next appointment, which was an afternoon of testing, including blood work; ultrasound; electromyography (EMG), which measured the activity of muscles and the motor neuron impulses that control them; and an electroencephalogram (EEG) was used to measure electrical activity in the brain. There was no pain and we were optimistic that the nerve could be released from its trap.

The doctor's office called and requested that we both

attend the appointment where the results of the tests would be revealed. While we were nervous that the worst-case scenario would probably mean shoulder surgery, there was also some relief around finally having answers and a potential solution. Honestly, I was selfishly hoping that he would at least be able to keep on making home improvements. The rain had leaked through the roof above the kitchen window and a large piece of the ceiling was threatening to fall and crush my toddler at any moment.

Donovan announced that he was off for a run to clear the cobwebs before the appointment. "A run sounds great," I said. "I'll come." He stared at me in confusion before I gave in and said, "Oh, right! I'll stay with the baby, shall I?" He shook his head as if I'd lost my mind and closed the front door behind him. Note to self—find some passive-aggressive way to make a point later.

We pulled into a parking spot with one minute to spare. In an unprecedented move, the nurse showed us into an examination room with almost no waiting. Dr. Naisdar, unaffectionately known as "the late Dr. Naisdar," was running on time. So strange. The nurse asked Donovan to strip down to his boxers and sit on the examination table. He complied and I gave him a half-smile confused look. I thought this was a sit-across-the-desk-and-chat kind of an appointment. We were both giggling about how excessively hairy his toes were and how his thick black leg hair came to a dead stop at his ankles as if he were wearing hair trousers, when the doctor came in. We exchanged pleasantries and Donovan answered some basic "how are you feeling" questions while the doctor banged various parts of his body with a tiny mallet. He then rolled a wheelie stool beneath him and sat facing both of us.

"The test results were a little worse than expected."

Did he actually say the word little*?*

Donovan nodded. "We figured it wasn't great news when the receptionist asked for us both to come—is it surgery, Doc? Do I need an operation on the shoulder?"

The doctor inhaled deeply and released the air slowly through pursed lips, making his cheeks puff out as he did so.

"No, Donovan, no operation. I believe you have something called amyotrophic lateral sclerosis. Or Lou Gehrig's disease." We stared blankly with no clue of what this man was talking about. "It is a disease of the motor neurons." This didn't help . . . neither did the squinting I was doing in an attempt to comprehend.

"Wait. Didn't Lou Gehrig die?" Donovan asked.

"Who is Lou . . . ?" I grew up in Wales; we are a rugby nation, not baseball. I rested a hand on my husband's bare, hairy leg as I interjected, to reassure him, "And that is not what's happening to you."

I made a statement, but I looked at the doctor for confirmation.

"I'm afraid the news is very grim. ALS is a terminal illness with no treatment or cure. You will need to see a specialist, but I am fairly sure about this."

Kaboom.

"You have three to five years to live."

What the actual fuck did he just say? I continued to look at the doctor whose mouth was moving but the sound he was making was muffled as if he were talking underwater. *No. No. No. This cannot be.* I was confused. This must be wrong. I was *fairly sure* that this stupid doctor was wrong. I thought I might vomit.

Shut up. Shut the fuck up. I can't keep up. I don't know what's happening here.

I looked at my husband who was staring at me and shaking his head in disbelief. I cupped his face with my hands so we could focus on each other, so we could hear each other over the blur of confusion filling the examination room. I lied to him about how wrong this was, how we would see someone else, how this was clearly a mistake. I was vaguely aware of the doctor in the background, saying he understood how difficult this must be for us. Donovan looked up and the tears came as he laid his last card on the table.

"But I have a baby boy."

He pleaded with his doctor to reconsider the diagnosis and spare his life. The doctor answered with, "Listen, I am going to prescribe you something to take the edge off, but I need to know that you won't take too many, that you're not feeling suicidal." This added to Donovan's confusion and I felt my anger start to rise. My husband still sat in his underwear, on the edge of an examination table, his feet dangling, his head hung. He looked deflated, vulnerable, and unfamiliar. I had a brief vision of grabbing the doctor's face and squeezing his cheeks, digging in my fingernails until I broke through the skin and he came to his senses.

Instead, I asked him, "What makes you think he wants to accelerate the death sentence you just gave him?" I spat these words at Dr. Naisdar and started pressing clothes into Donovan for him to get dressed. He remained motionless, but I needed to flee that office. The doctor excused himself to give us a moment of privacy; he couldn't stand to watch us unravel for one more second. I snapped Donovan out of a trance; he looked up but not at me, more through me. I told him it was time to go and he dressed—but the vacant expression remained. We drove home in silence, picked up Donovan-Rhys, and said nothing of the news. The words had only just gone in. They would have to be absorbed and understood before sending them back out to attack family and friends. We read the tri-folded pamphlet given to us by the nurse and did some research. This neurodegenerative disease, also known as a motor neuron disease, will slowly cause the muscles of the body to break down, rendering the person unable to walk, talk, eat, swallow, and then breathe. There was no glimmer of hope, no aggressive treatment plan or 50/50 surgery for us to pin our hopes on. There simply was no hope. Unacceptable. We sat with the finality of the information that we could not grasp or understand. Then Donovan said the only thing that made sense.

"I am obviously too young for this disease. Before we throw in the towel, we should probably consider the possibility that this diagnosis is wrong."

Yes. *I love this idea.* We had seen one doctor. ONE! And

what did he know? I agreed and we wiped our red eyes before we wasted any more tears on this hurtful and negligent medical mistake. We wrote off Dr. Naisdar as irresponsible and heartless for this outrageous and false diagnosis. We planned second, better, opinions and coached ourselves back down to earth.

Welcome to step one: denial.

With a small sentence, in a small room, the diagnosis of ALS was delivered. I'm not sure if there was another way—or even a better way—to hear that news but I do know that the vastness of those words didn't fit in that room, or in our lives. What I know now is that those words were the tip of an incomprehensible iceberg, and we were about to start a journey that would reveal the enormity of what was hidden under the surface.

CHAPTER 5

Death Notification— Level: Expert

ON DEATH DAY MY HUSBAND and I had two boys: nine-year-old Donovan-Rhys, named after his dad, and seven-year-old Dylan, my Welsh choice. They weren't home when their dad died. The evening before, I decided to send them to my best friend Sue's place. Before Sue moved, only a shared chain-link fence divided our two backyards. We installed a matching gate on one end because it was safer than passing kids back and forth across the six-foot-high fence. It was also safer than leaning a ladder against the fence from either side for drunken adults to run home and check on sleeping children. (Save the sanctimony, folks—that was the '90s.)

Sue and I had a home-based day care so we could make money while staying home with our respective kids—and so I could stay home and take care of my terminally ill husband. We spent most days together taking our little ones to the park, a church playgroup, or each other's yards. She had a strict "no kids in the house unless your mom is paying me" policy, which made her house a mystical castle of forbidden toys. In their preschool days, the boys would play on Sue's deck and try to breach the perimeter.

"Where are you off to, mister?" she'd ask.

"I have to pee," one of them would say, grabbing his shorts.

"There is a bathroom at your house, buddy. You can run home. I'll time you."

"I don't need to go anymore." Defeat.

There was, however, one breach. Not on Sue's watch, but when her husband, Blaine, was on guard. Blaine would patiently talk to Donovan-Rhys for what seemed like hours at a time, while Donovan swung on his swing, blankie tucked firmly under his arm, jerking his swing set so hard that both the front and then the back legs would leave the ground. He would maintain this perfect rhythm while he solved the problems of the world with Blaine. Donovan thought that Blaine was his best friend and one day made an earnest request to visit the prohibited household.

Blaine finally caved and said, "Sure, buddy. You can come play in our yard."

I came outside to find Blaine lying on his deck, peering through the panes in the bottom of the door, shouting, "Hey, buddy, how about you unlock the door and let Blaine in?"

This visit, I had thought, would subsequently make them jump up and down in excitement to visit Sue's new place and they'd be arguing about who would sleep where. But no, they were reluctant, even when I made promises of the GOOD breakfast cereal.

When they left that evening, I was pretty sure that it would be the last time they saw their dad. We all were. I think that somehow the boys knew it too. Or maybe it was the extra "I love you" and the longer hugs. I figured they knew something was up. I expected that Sue would do all the right things and take the best care of them; she always did. But in the years to follow, I struggled with the decision I made to send them away for the night. Should I have let the boys stay? Should I have allowed them to see their dad's dead body? Is that a normal part of acceptance and healing that I robbed them of? The generic experts say that a child should be given the choice. They should decide their own level of participation in the death process; it will help them to feel even a minor sense of control in an overwhelming situation. I have to wonder if these experts had children of their own; specifically, seven- and nine-year-old boys.

Decision-making was not their strong suit. Donovan-Rhys once chose to ask his brother to dunk his head under their shared bathwater to see if fart bubbles smelled under the surface. Dylan chose to give it a go and promptly filled his lungs with dirty, fart-imbued water. On another occasion, while playing hide-and-seek, Dylan chose to conceal himself in the chest freezer we kept in the shed. One of the most creative choices Donovan-Rhys came up with was to shove his baby brother in the dryer and close the door, which made me scream the following: "Jesus! I can't even take a shit in peace without impending death happening to the both of you!"

Just to set the scene, I had shrieked this in front of a man standing at the screen door, who had just arrived to adjust Donovan's power wheelchair. Honestly, I could go on all day about the "choices" my little boys made.

I told myself that I did the very best I could with what I knew at that time. Yet the gut-wrenching image of ushering my boys out of the house holding the hands of another mummy stuck to me like the lingering smell of a damp towel.

About a million and sixteen years later, I asked the boys about their last memory of their dad.

The first time I had this conversation with Donovan-Rhys, he replied to this question something like this: "I was sitting cross-legged on his bed; Scruffy dog was up there too. The Toronto Maple Leafs were playing on TV and there were a lot of friends over. I guess they were saying goodbye. Dad was tired but he smiled anyway. He talked to me, but I couldn't hear or make out what he said, so I said 'Okay, Dad' a lot, and told him that I loved him. I think he was telling me to be a good boy. Sorry I didn't listen."

He'd laugh, and then cry. And so did I.

Dylan didn't really remember being shipped off to Sue's at all. He recalls a lot of people, and he remembers that they were all nice to him. His memories don't have a defined chronological order, but he did have a favorite.

"I was standing on the back of Dad's wheelchair. He was taking me to Edward's Park, maybe for T-ball. When we were crossing the field, he said, 'Hold on tight, Son,' and he went fast over the grass. It was bumpy and we went so fast that my hat came off. We laughed and went back for it then went really fast again. Dad told me not to tell you because you'd go on about safety. So, we kept it a secret."

I exhaled a breath I had been holding onto for far too long and forgave myself for the decisions I never wanted to make.

The last memories of their dad were exactly right.

The day of Donovan's death, I knew I had a momentous task ahead of me—to deliver the news to the boys. However, I felt I was well practiced for this moment. The boys had been in pre-grief counseling for months. Twice weekly, they were dragged off to sit with a specialist who dealt with preparing children for grief by drawing pictures depicting life cycles, and talking about where feelings live in the body. Dylan thought it was pretty cool to be allowed to draw dead things and blood, and then got in trouble for that at school. Donovan-Rhys protested before every appointment and then couldn't stop talking once he got there, so the groundwork had been laid. Just a quick limber up and I was ready to do this.

But I was *not* ready. I spent a moment screaming "FUCK!" at my steering wheel before getting out of the car at the school. Kate and I walked just close enough so that we could peer through the heavy, double doors of the school office. Two little boys with oversized backpacks sat waiting, dangling their feet from a pile of stackable chairs. They were watching the secretary cry because she already knew. A wave of anger washed over me, and I suddenly hated everything and everyone. I especially hated little children who had the audacity to have a healthy dad. I hated that I had to deliver this life-defining news—and I was really fucking angry that I couldn't protect them from the pain of it.

We waved them out to the car.

That was where they were told that their dad had died. Dylan let out a small, nervous laugh and his brother snapped that it wasn't funny. Seeing the guilt on my little boy's face felt like I was being stabbed straight through the heart.

"It's okay, babe—sometimes the feeling is so big, we can't control how we express it."

Stabbed in the heart also depicted the look of guilt on my bigger little boy's face for making his younger brother feel bad on the day their dad died.

"Sweetheart, you did nothing wrong."

Holy shit! I hadn't considered the possibility that this could go even worse than anticipated. Surely, it was already as bad as it could get . . . I was acutely aware that little boys lash out before acknowledging feelings, so it was time to gather the reins. I told them that this was new for all of us, and that we were all on our first day and we would learn how to do this together. We would be gentle and understanding with each other as we experienced huge, overpowering new feelings. They looked at me, searching for comfort. For the relief, and the words that would make up for the bomb I had dropped on them—the "but" that would serve as a compromise and soften the blow.

But I didn't have it to give.

So I picked up a McDonald's Happy Meal at the drive-through for them both.

The tears came as the boys walked through the door of our little house. The incomprehensible words I had spoken in the car were confirmed by the absence of a hospital bed, machines, and a daddy. I watched Dylan's hands ball into fists as the pain of loss and the anger of desperation moved through him.

There were so many tasks that needed to be completed throughout the day. Despite wanting to do anything other than visit a funeral home or have phone conversations or think about what we would eat for dinner, those things were accomplished with a robotic numbness. These chores were periodically interrupted with waves of sadness that could, in retrospect, make a mountain crumble. The to-do list was surprisingly long, and someone should seriously figure out a way to delay the necessities of death, at least for a day. Could we just have those first hours to wander around in a daze repeating, "I can't believe it"?

Ultimately, we completed the assignments and got through the challenges of Death Day, ground zero. That evening, I pulled my boys in close and sat with my family. We struggled to comprehend how monumental the day had been. How the finality of death is easy to understand in a literal sense, but impossible to fathom in the face of it. It felt bigger than all of us, but we sat together and unwound. We shared stories and laughed. We reveled in the memories and then we made fun of my sister for being an ugly crier. We felt hollow and fragile, but the truth was, we had never been so strong. There was never a choice but to get through that day. But the lack of choice in the matter didn't detract from the love and dedication it took to do it. Preparation was not the key. It was years of building resilience in the face of overwhelming heartache, frustration, and exhaustion that made us all stronger than we knew.

It would be months later, while clearing closet space, when I came across the vacuum-sealed bag with Donovan's pillow squished inside. I sat with it on my lap and reeled from the rush of memories it generated. I instantly felt that familiar lump in my throat, along with the ache of loss. I would do anything to drink in that smell and remember my husband. I sat on the floor and picked at the plastic closure, crying in anticipation before I pulled open the zip—just a little at first, but not too far. Enough to bask in the pain but not enough to let all the "smell-memory" out. I readied myself with a big exhale and buried my face into the opening.

Inhale ... The second it hit me, I nearly vomited. It was putrid! I pulled my face away and dry-heaved. As I turned the bag over and stared at some unfamiliar markings, I realized that what I was looking at was mildew that had literally *flowered*, sprouting its charming black blooms all over the surface. It took me a second to figure out why my pillow preservation had failed. The realization of my stupidity slowly washed over me and I started to chuckle as my sister poked her head in to see what was amusing and repulsing me in equal measure.

"Jesus, Mary, and Irene. What the fuck is that smell?!" She was similarly assaulted by the stench.

At this point I was laughing; really laughing. There were also tears, but they could have been from retching. My sister grabbed the bag and rolled the top down while walking it to the rubbish bin and calling me an idiot between gagging noises. Later that evening, Kate presented me with a small angel pin, which was deftly retrieved from the end of the pillow through the bag, ever so carefully, so she wouldn't get pillow mold on her arm.

The effort was truly appreciated.

CHAPTER 6

Take the Pill, Woman

THE TERMINALLY ILL SET PARAMETERS to protect themselves and the ones they love by creating an emotional force field to ward off excess feelings. They might make plans "for when they're better" or even pretend their illness is nonexistent. They might withhold love; they might require more control, or they might need to pull back. They may have a clear vision of what changes should be made to make room for their diagnosis. Sometimes, those parameters are for people who don't even exist. In our home, a decision was made about whether or not we were to have more children and I was not invited to participate in the decision-making process.

Following his diagnosis, Donovan made that decision. *Why the fuck would we choose to create a life, knowing that the child would, at some point, become a fatherless semi-orphan?* This was a fact. Spoiler alert: Donovan died. But isn't there risk involved anyway? Even the healthiest of parents could succumb to some unseen, unexpected illness or disaster. At any point, any one of us could be hit by a bus or die in a fiery crash and the result would be the same. But would you have another child if you knew that bus was headed your way?

I understood his decision—but I also wanted a voice. I wanted to be heard, but it was hard to shout over the noise of terminal illness.

I was *supposed* to have three children. That was part of the grand plan. My son Donovan-Rhys was about a year and a half old when my husband, Donovan, was diagnosed with ALS. That diagnosis was not only a life sentence for him, but it was also the end of making babies for us both. We could practice, of course; we would still have a few years left before being robbed of our physical ability. But more babies? That was a hard *no*. My husband's hard no. I mourned the loss of children I would never conceive while being told I should "count my blessings" because "some women don't even get one." I would nod and agree. I was, indeed, a lucky girl.

The anger of injustice is a complex disaster. It is visceral. The frantic grasp for control made me demand to speak to an imagined manager—to bang my fist on the desk and demand an answer as to why I couldn't have more babies. But who would be able provide that insight?

I had no answer, because by this point, God and I were no longer on speaking terms.

As a baby, Donovan-Rhys was challenging. He cried a lot. I cried along with him. We struggled with breastfeeding, bonding, colic, and the sleep deprivation was exhausting. I was unprepared for the beginning stages of motherhood. And side bar—no one told me how sore my arse would be following three hours of pushing and a forceps delivery, nor did anyone inform me that my nipples would be so sore they would bruise. The way I came to that lovely conclusion was, shockingly, when a nurse on the maternity floor rolled in a cart with a double breast pump on it. She announced that it was "time to get some juices flowing" so we could "stop that baby from crying." I was subsequently milked. Yes, milked, like a cow. I was involuntarily hooked up to a machine that stretched my nipples longer than scientifically feasible. In retrospect, I am pretty sure she pulled a cord to start it like a lawn mower. Worse still, my husband showed up for a visit at that precise moment and I had to shout over the noise of the lawn mower / milking machine engine. Donovan assured me that nothing could be as bad as watching the delivery (uh ... thanks?), so I went on to clarify the situation by describing my nipples as long, skinny dicks being rhythmically stretched into test tubes, producing little to no results.

Donovan said he would wait outside.

Once home, things didn't improve. I didn't know that it was okay to put a crying baby down so I carried him all the time—but he cried anyway. Sometimes, I would put him in a bouncy chair on the floor of the bathroom so I could shower, which wasn't often, because my baby never stopped screaming. I went days without showering, acutely aware that I smelled of breast milk, spit-up, and my own unshaved armpits. At the baby's six-week checkup, I inquired about the return policy—but followed it up with a fake laugh so the doctor would never know if I was actually serious. The doctor told me that breastfeeding was "the most natural thing in the world," and that women had, in fact, been doing it for centuries, or possibly longer. He also thought I should try to be more like my sisters-in-law. Just be like them! Stop crying, whining, and do the stuff and the things. And, for fuck's sake, feed this underweight, hungry baby! Breasts are made for feeding an infant, so just do it. *Get your shit together, slacker. Anyone can be a mother!* This is not a direct quote, but his opinion of my crappy mothering skills was very clear. How the hell did I even make it onto his roster?

My family was thousands of miles away in Wales. So, I looked to, and up to, my sisters-in-law. The women whom I wanted to be my friends and who I thought were my friends—my husband's sisters. They seemed to have it all together. They were good mothers, kept a clean house, and did all the things my doctor talked about. I felt judged; so I tried harder and messed up more. I wanted to fit in with this family and be like them. Except, I couldn't keep up. My husband worked afternoons and followed an uninterruptible sleep, video-game, and workout schedule. So we stayed home, the two of us: a red-faced screaming alien that I didn't particularly like and a newly stretch-marky me, who I liked much less. I felt weak, incapable, broken, and like a failure. I lived in fear of having my baby taken away because of my inadequacies. I sneaked him formula and lied about it. At night, I would lie on my bed with my head at the foot end because that is where the windup swing was. Donovan-Rhys would only sleep in the swing, while it was swinging. But it would only swing for fifteen minutes before requiring a windup again. I would hear him groan and squirm as the swing slowed and I would lean over the edge of the bed to get it going again before the groan turned into the inconsolable screams, as it so often did. Every moment of every day was spent trying to get the baby to sleep. On one occasion, I laid him down for a nap after cry rocking (both of us) and bouncing for hours. He finally fell asleep, and I gently laid him down, patting his bum while holding his dummy in before I silently tiptoed out of his room like a cartoon character, avoiding anything that creaked. I made it all the way downstairs, put on the kettle, and sat in front of a basket of laundry to fold. Would this finally be the tea I get to drink hot?

Nope, no it wouldn't.

He let out a scream at the nine-minute mark and I joined in. I threw onesies all over the floor and poured my tea down the sink before climbing back up the stairs. I made my way up to his room, gripping the banister hard enough to break two nails and biting my lip until I tasted blood. I didn't know if I was going to pick up my infant and console him or if I was going to throw him out of a second-story window.

Yup, I said that out loud. Did you hear it?

I actually didn't know if I would throw my baby out of a window. Would you mind keeping that to yourself? We inadequate mothers already have enough shame; we don't need the extra judgment. Exhale. Of course, I didn't throw him. I also didn't *want* to hurt him but, in that moment, desperation and exhaustion made thoughts and actions independent of each other. They told me lies about my worth that I believed. They robbed me of my me-ness. In the past, I had judged mothers who made headline news by hurting their babies. Now, I understood how some of them reached that point. More frightening, this unhinging went largely unnoticed. While in the middle of it, I had no idea that this could be anything more than my own character flaw. When I could no longer muster the energy to smile and lie about being fine, I simply withdrew and hid away. Donovan did know that something wasn't quite right. There was no actual conversion, so he chalked it up to homesickness and tried to cheer me up with a puppy for my birthday.

However, Donovan-Rhys was four months old, and my husband already had an untrained, destructive, hyperactive boxer dog. A puppy was not going to lighten my burden and I couldn't keep it.

The day Donovan-Rhys turned six months, I executed a devious plan that I had secretly and cunningly been thinking about for a month. (Cue dramatic music, please.) That night, I put him down in his crib, with a bottle . . . of formula. This bottle was propped on a blanket that I scrunched in front of his face to keep that sucker from rolling away. Dentists and Le Leche League members from around the world developed spontaneous eye twitches as I abandoned all hopes of straight teeth for my infant, by providing poor nutrition and the inability to fight infection—along with my acceptance of a lifelong membership to "The Bad Mum's Club."

That momentous day, my baby slept through the night. I, of course, did not. I lay awake thinking that obviously he had died because of terrible mothering. But I couldn't check because what if he was actually sleeping and I woke him up?

Gahhhh!

The monitor picked up a foreign babbling sound in the morning and I ran to his room wondering why he wasn't screaming. He was awake—but he wasn't crying. I think the accurate description would be—he awoke content but it was too unfamiliar to recognize. I enjoyed this little win and assumed it was a "never to be repeated fluke" and prepared to continue battling this crying monster into adulthood.

But it wasn't a fluke.

That morning, at six months and one day old, I met my son for the first time and soon fell head over heels in love. The fog lifted, and the undiagnosed postpartum depression subsided with rest. I then came to terms with the big fat side order of parenting guilt that came with his birth and infancy instructional package that, frankly, I should have paid more attention to. (It also would have been useful to have the heads-up about how sore, post-delivery, I would be. No, still not over it.)

My baby boy became a thick, damp, giggling drooler who not only forgave me for fucking up the beginning of our story together, but I think he actually forgot about it.

At least, he never brings it up. His teeth were fine, and he is immuno-fine. Everything was, at that moment, fine.

Until it wasn't.

I hadn't considered the impact Donovan's ALS diagnosis would have on our decision to have children. I thought that the plan would continue as originally conceived. I hadn't considered that we wouldn't be having a baby when we had a toddler, then another when the second baby was a toddler. The answer was, "How could you even think about having another baby now!?" (*You idiot.*) Yes, I added the last bit—only to demonstrate the tone in which it was delivered. The decision was so obvious, and I was the only one questioning it. I accepted the decision. What was I supposed to say?

Let me try ...

"No, terminally ill husband. Who bestowed infinite wisdom on you?? I demand you put a baby in there right now!" One of us had to concede here, and only one of us held the terminally ill trump card. I was already taking birth control and that was that. The Pill, for life; or until sex became a distant memory and my vagina closed over and I became an unwilling born-again virgin.

When I went to my (new and amazing) family doctor to inquire if there was anything that may help with mid-cycle bleeding, she suggested a prescription change. "No big deal—take this new pill on the first day of your next period."

Sure. Easy peasy. If I ever *had* a first day of my next period. I mean, I did have a next period but not until after the birth of my second son—and after I had stopped a year of breastfeeding. Of course, once the shock of an unplanned pregnancy subsided, Donovan loved his second son, Dylan, long before he appeared in this world—and more than he ever thought possible.

Great! Congratulations on having a toddler, a terminally ill husband, a naughty Jack Russell terrier, and a newborn. Are you happy now? Well, actually, yes, I was.

And no.

But yes.

Okay, so this is no one's ideal situation. But my newborn, Dylan, got the message that an easygoing disposition would be super handy. He was put to the test on his first day home, which was actually after a nine-day stint in the ICU to ward off a bout of RSV. He was jaundiced on the day we were to go home but I begged the doctor to discharge him, promising that I would lay him in the sunlight of the window and bring him in every day for a bilirubin test.

Success!

The kid was sprung, and we were homeward bound. Day one at home, I thought, *I've got this*. My husband went out with his dad, and my toddler went down for his nap. My mum, visiting from Wales, was taking a moment to read, while Dylan and I napped in the playroom. As promised, my baby was naked except for a diaper, in a bassinet on the floor, sunbathing in the beam of sunlight coming through the window. I was on the couch. Mum popped her head in and asked if I wanted tea. She left to put the kettle on, and I went to the bathroom. In that short period of time, my toddler instinctually woke in time for *Blue's Clues*. He and his stuffed monkey made their way to the playroom. He then proceeded to take Dylan out of the bassinet and put him on the floor. He replaced the real baby with Monkey.

Mum gasped a little as she poked her head around the corner, which caused Donovan-Rhys to panic. He threw Monkey out, lifted Dylan by his diaper, and tossed him back in. Dylan didn't even wake up. Chill baby test passed with flying colors.

There would be plenty of tests and many fails—and plenty of times where I thought the one failing was me. But Dylan settled into a contentment that I was sure was some sort of secret gift. He was patient. And he was a pro at helping himself to boob while in a sling. He did wake in the night to feed until he was thirteen months, but honestly, I loved that time where it was just he and I. We would sit in his room, and he would look up at me and giggle with a milky grin, and I would remind him that, "It's time for eating, not smiling, mister." He would fall asleep while attached to me and I loved every sleep-interrupted moment.

Go ahead; make a judgment call or have a strong opinion on whether I should have brought a child into the world knowing that his dad would die. Knowing that he might be heartbreakingly sad, confused, and angry at the world at some point. Maybe I shouldn't have. Or . . . maybe death, and the destruction and sadness it brings upon us, can be a part of living, when it has to be. Maybe death has moments of joy, celebration, and growth. That is what I chose—to let love rule over fear and to nurture our little family. It was hard; it was wonderful, tiring, and rewarding. You know, like every struggling young family.

For our family, ALS had moved in and taken a permanent place at our table. It was demanding and loud-mouthed and took up way too much space. But eventually we trained it to speak when spoken to and share our space with all the happiness we could muster, along with the demands that beautiful little boys have. Maybe, ALS could take a very long hike while we wrestled and built Legos—and while we read those cool books. The fact is that my boys brought enough joy to make the sadness bearable. Children don't let sadness take up all of their space. They experience the feeling then put it down to watch cartoons. We should attempt to learn all we can from the tiny humans, because honestly, they are much smarter than we are when it comes to this stuff. Maybe then we could find balance. Just add equal parts joy to the sadness that lives within us and meet that bitch head-on.

CHAPTER 7

Cremation Socks

MY HUSBAND DIED YESTERDAY.

My. Husband. Died. Yesterday. I am a . . . wiiddoowww.

I rolled the words around in my mouth, seeing how they tasted, trying them out. They didn't feel real and they didn't suit me. I was thirty years old. How the fuck was I a widow?

Also, whose idea was it to pair spousal death with major decision-making? Funeral decisions. Financial decisions. What's-for-dinner decisions. On top of that, keep the small humans alive. I couldn't think about anything except Donovan's death. I replayed it on a continuous loop and worried that I had already forgotten key details—like socks.

Yesterday, on the day my husband died, I went to a local funeral home to make important decisions that I was in no state of mind to make. One of the conversations I had with the funeral people was around the cremation. The funeral lady asked if I had thought about what Donovan would be wearing.

I was confused.

"Wearing? For what?" Yup, I asked that out loud.

"His last outfit, the clothes he will be cremated in." She smiled as she said it but her eyes told me that she wondered what kind of idiot sat across from her. She was probably thinking that I was the exact person who needed the "It's hot" warning on a coffee take-out cup. She had lipstick on her teeth, though, so at least there's that.

"Oh, right, of course." I offered this lie as if I had momentarily forgotten about the cremation. "Yes, it's all planned. I will drop it down to you this afternoon." Shit, now I'd lied to the people in charge of cremating my husband. I would undoubtedly be stubbing my toe at some point later that day. It does seem like an awful lot of unnecessary effort, though. Undressing a dead person to redress them in some-thing clean, likely awkward, and possibly too small to cre-mate them? There would be no viewing or visitation, so what was the point? I wondered, in my slightly demented state of mind, if in situations like this they just toss the clothes in there with the body. I wouldn't blame them.

All of Donovan's clothes had been modified after he was diagnosed. He lost the dexterity of his hands early on in the ALS disease process. Buttons were one of his first sacrifices, quickly followed by the dreaded zip. His jeans were replaced with elastic-waist, pull-on-style pants that were stretchy and comfy and dignity-diminishing. The shirts were but-ton-free. Initially, all of this was done to facilitate some independence. He could walk himself to the bathroom, but the trouser button was a fucker. Exchanging the button for elastic meant he was able to slip his thumbs inside the waist of his pants and slide them up and down. It wasn't long before the benefit was for the person dressing him, when hooking his thumbs became a game of chance and when he could no longer reliably lift his hands to waist height or could no longer safely walk to the bathroom. We kept "real" clothes that he wore on special occasions: a suit, a pair of jeans with a zipper, and a button-down shirt.

I walked into the house, post-funeral planning, announcing: "I have to take an outfit down for Donovan." I paused for dramatic effect. "To be cremated in," I clarified. I made this announcement to my mother, Kate, and Jonathan, expecting a reaction. I thought it would provoke something to the effect of, "What on earth for?" Or, "Well, that's a waste of decent clothing." But . . . nope. Nothing. They just stared at me, grief-stricken from the morning's events.

"Have you thought about what he'll wear?" Mum asked as if this were both normal and anticipated.

"Um. Not really; this was a little unexpected." I was shocked at their lack of shocked indignation. I was less shocked when Jonathan suggested, "Oooh, I know—why don't you drop off a dominatrix outfit, for a laugh, like. It would be hilarious!" While I agreed in principle, I didn't have one on hand. I wondered out loud if he was supposed to be in a suit. My sister thought that would be a great choice if I wanted to be haunted by an angry, itchy ghost of Donovan that would leave small Lego pieces underfoot for the rest of my life. The fabulous thing was that not even the subject of cremation could cause the family sarcasm to skip a beat. I left this most unhelpful conversation and wandered into what used to be our bedroom. I shimmied open the sticky bottom drawer of Donovan's dresser. I had found the dresser on the curb; someone had put it out for bulk garbage day. I refinished it and put on new handles, but the bottom drawer never opened smoothly so that is where the unmodified, rarely worn clothes were kept. I pulled out a pair of Levi's as Dylan came in to see what I was doing.

"I have to find some clothes for your dad to wear."

Dylan crumpled up his face as he tried to wrap his brain around this. "Huh?"

"Right," I agreed. "I'm with you, Dyl. I don't get it either, but the funeral people think that Dad should have a forever outfit. Want to help pick one?" He shrugged and nodded in agreement that this was a good idea. I pulled him down into my cross-legged lap to combine decision-making with a snuggle.

"What is he wearing right now?" Clearly, my son needed a baseline.

"Jammie bottoms and a T-shirt that came free with a case of beer."

"He doesn't want to be in those forever. He would like jeans. The real kind, like mine." He demonstrated by pulling the waist of his jeans out to show the button.

"Yes. That's what I was thinking. What about on top?"

Dylan pushed himself free of me and went to our tiny, shared closet. He yanked on one side of a shirt, causing the hanger to pop out of the shoulder and bounce off the roof of the closet. He outstretched his arm and declared, "That one." It was his dad's official National Hockey League, Toronto Maple Leafs jersey, emblazoned with the number

13 for his favorite player, Mats Sundin. "That shirt made him cry at Christmas, but happy cry because he loves it."

"Dylan! I knew you were a genius. This is the most perfect outfit. It is exactly what your dad would want to wear. Thank you for helping; now I won't have to step on Lego forever." Dylan frowned and walked off.

It crossed my mind for a split second that I was about to burn the most expensive shirt I had ever purchased. The jersey was a shockingly expensive Christmas present that I'd saved up to buy Donovan. Then it crossed my mind that I was probably going to step on Lego forever for even contemplating the cost of my husband's cremation shirt. I walked out to the kitchen to stuff the clothes into a plastic bag for transport when my mother stopped me, insisting on ironing them before I left. I put up the following weak argument: Jeans don't need ironing. Especially when they are going to be burned.

She countered with, "No son-in-law of mine is being cremated in creased jeans." Definitely a solid argument. Neatly pressed and folded jeans were hung over the bar of a hanger under a neatly pressed hockey jersey, which was then hung on the little fold-down hook next to the "oh shit" handle in the back of my car. I drove the clothes down to the funeral home where a young attendant took them from me, and without looking at the clothes, added that he thought "the deceased" would look very nice. I wanted to punch him in the throat for calling Donovan "the deceased."

The following morning, after realizing that, yes, this was all actually happening, I forced myself out of bed to contemplate the enormity of everything and put the previous day's events into some kind of manageable order. While I stared into my tea, I imagined answers would float to the top. I thought of the young man at the funeral home who had the audacity to call Donovan "the deceased." That made me think of the cremation outfit. That led to me to thinking . . . OH MY GOOD GOD . . . socks!! I was stunned by this most horrid realization; I hadn't packed any socks for Donovan! I felt the color drain from my face as I burst into tears. My family gathered around, ready to help—or to tell me I am an idiot—whatever was needed. I reached for the phone and dialed the number for the funeral home to ask if the cremation had taken place. It had. The cremation technician recorded the start time as 8:11, which was forty-eight minutes earlier. I hung up and wept into my tea as I tried to turn the squeaking sob noises into words. When I finally formed a sentence, I confessed the oversight to my patient but bewildered family.

My sister, clearly underestimating my distress, asked if I had remembered shoes. I blew my nose into a tissue and assured her that, obviously, the dead do not need shoes. But Donovan always had cold feet, and now he was doomed to spend the whole of eternity chilly and sockless. Jonathan was kind enough to point out that Donovan's feet were literally on fire as we were speaking and not the least bit chilly. Mum casually poured boiling water into her mug then pushed the floating tea bag to the bottom with a spoon while saying, "You're not crying over socks, love. Yesterday you didn't even think he needed clothes." Of course, she was right. How did she always know how my brain worked? I was a one-day-old widow; therefore I was allowed to cry over whatever I wanted. Socks included. Mum also thought that there was a better foot cover option.

"You should have taken his non-slip booties, the ones that I made. That would have been a better choice. You never know what type of flooring he'll be walking on, and he loved those slippers."

"That's ridiculous," Kate piped in. "He won't need to non-slip anything. He won't have ALS anymore. He will be a healthy Donovan. He will probably need hockey skates, not shoes."

"He was always a better spectator than a player. Weak ankles, you see," I reminded her.

"Why on earth would he be free of ALS but still be plagued with weak ankles?" Fair point from my sister.

The conversation continued and the boys joined in. They were filled with ideas about what their dad could do now. Maybe he was strong, maybe he could lift a little boy high above him, maybe he could wrestle. Soon there were crayons out and pictures being drafted of a superhero dad, a flying dad, a hockey-playing dad, a dad catching a ball, and a dad walking all by himself. Something Dylan could not remember ever seeing, which is probably why in one of his drawings, his dad was flying, cape flowing behind him while still sitting in a wheelchair. My family, once again, in their weird and wonderful way, talked me off the edge of a self-loathing rabbit hole. The negative self-talk was exchanged for sarcasm and a little teasing, which was to be expected, and, in all honesty, had been earned. Happy Donovan talk ensued. This felt good. I wanted the easy way we included Donovan in everyday conversation to last forever, sharing memories and never being afraid to mention him for fear of upsetting one another. Talking about Donovan allowed him to remain present and a part of our lives. If there were tears, it was because they were due, not because they were provoked by bringing him up in conversation.

I hoped that the boys would say, "How would Daddy do it?" and "What did Daddy like on his pizza?" and a million other questions about Donovan that popped into their confused little heads. I hoped he stayed with us always, remaining a part of our daily lives and conversation, perpetually a part of our love for each other.

I'm still regretful about his cold feet.

CHAPTER 8

The Devil Loves Desperation

THERE IS A FINE LINE between desperation and hope. Hope is the belief that something good will emerge. Hope for a positive outcome, a groundbreaking treatment, or even a cure. Desperation, for us, was upholding an ever-present sense of hope. Searching, investing time, energy—and money that we didn't have—into an exhaustive quest for an answer that would give us back the time we were wasting. It would also, ostensibly, give us back the time we wasted while engaged in the original fruitless search. Desperation was one of the non-physical deficits ALS inflicted upon us. One of the disease symptoms that I suffered from, despite not actually having the ailment.

There are some crappy people in the world, and some were right in my neighborhood. I would imagine they might exist in yours too. I do believe that most people are fundamentally good and occasionally those good people do cruel things. There are also extra crappy people who intentionally do crappy things and are basically a waste of breathable air. I have had the misfortune to experience both.

When Donovan's hands could no longer be relied upon to work the joystick that controlled his power wheelchair, it was modified. The control was placed on the footrest, and he would learn to drive using his feet. This adaptation was both genius and terrifying. Donovan's only source of independence and freedom was his chair. When he first got it, he practiced in the backyard, taking off so quickly that both the technician and occupational therapist responsible for fitting him chased after him, one after the other shouting, "Let go of the toggle!" All that was missing from the moment was the *Benny Hill* theme as the pursuit weaved its way through the garden.

When he ventured out alone, I followed from a distance, surreptitiously trying to stay incognito so I wouldn't suffer his wrath when I got busted. When he was proficient, he went on daily outings, often with Donovan-Rhys riding on the back and Dylan sitting on his dad's lap. Donovan became well known in our town and planned to meet every resident while on his travels. When he learned to drive using his foot, I once again had the urge to follow him and he knew that I would so he warned me off. I said, "No promises," and he threatened to mow me down in the street with his chair if he caught me lurking from afar. He headed off down the ramp that led from our deck out to the street and promptly drove straight into the side of the neighbor's house, scraping his arm on the pebble dash.

"Okay, got it now," he assured me, and left. I waited a few moments and obviously followed. About three blocks away, Donovan lost control and drove his chair off the curb. The chair wobbled and tittered before tipping over on King Street, the main drag that ran through our town. When I got to him, he was on his side, lying on the road still in the chair with his arm trapped beneath it. He was fully obstructing traffic and people traveling in the lane had been driving around him. Yes, that's what I said, *driving around him*. Vehicles drove *around* a clearly disabled man lying in the road, obviously in need of help. And none of those idiots stopped. I arrived as one such person drove by and I screamed, "What the fuck is wrong with you?!" The next person stopped and was kind and helpful. He may have heard my delicate cry for help, or he might have been the one good person in twenty. The thing is, the twenty drive-byers probably are good people, too, who, for a host of reasons, did a crappy thing. I forgive you, you dicks. I hope you all developed an inexplicable burning crotch itch that evening and your "nether-regions" developed a foul scent that took a month to clear up.

While at the hospital for a team appointment with the ALS clinic, Donovan and I were sitting in the waiting room when we met a very nice lady who we discovered had a mother who had been living with ALS for two years.

We exchanged pleasantries and stories. I told her about my children. She explained that her mother was actually *doing great*. For her, the disease progression seemed to have halted. There had even been some reversal of symptoms and she and the family were feeling optimistic. Optimistic? How? What was she doing? I needed her to tell us everything, immediately if not sooner. We hungrily gobbled up every word she spoke, asking questions about balance and grip strength, speech and swallowing. This lady was doing well in all areas by using a combination of traditional Western management of symptoms, herbal supplements, and the alternative approach of a "laying on of hands" healer. We had to know more. We *had* to try this too. Unfortunately, this doctor of alternative healing was in high demand, and getting an appointment was unlikely. We took a spare card that this lady, Julia, had in her bag and I was in tears as I hugged her goodbye and thanked her for this glimmer of hope. I got Donovan into the car before the excitement burst. I squished his face between my fists and planted a kiss right on his smacker.

This might be it!

We called right away only to find that Julia was right—this man was booked solid for months. Damn, he must be good. I made an appointment for later in the year and added Donovan to a cancellation list. The cost of this treatment wasn't covered by provincial or private insurance, but the time frame meant we could save over the coming months. It was expensive, and money was tight. At that point, I was working three jobs—day care during the day,

Sears Portrait Studio in the evening, and as a waitress at an all-you-can-eat buffet on the weekend—and there was still more month left at the end of the money.

(Confession: I was a terrible waitress. Like really bad. I would bring people the wrong drink, then flirt and tell them, "Oh, you just look like you'd enjoy this more." Once, this perfectly nice lady asked me for a glass of Merlot. I forgot *three times*. When I was finally running her wine to her, a toddler busted free from her daddy and I made a quick but spilly stop to avoid her. I'd already made eye contact with "Wine Lady," so I hid at my station and poured the spilled wine from my serving tray back into her glass. Then I gave it to her. I will spare you the details of what goes on a serving tray and what it's wiped with. Not my proudest moment. Phew... that was a load off. Thanks for listening!)

We would find the stupid money. This was far more important. This was *hope*, people. A glimmer of hope!

When the phone rang the next day, the last thing I was expecting was an offer of an appointment with the healer. There was an opening for the following day and this poor receptionist had called everyone on the lengthy cancellation list, but because of the short notice, the appointment remained unfilled. I was already saying yes, of course we would take it, while trying to work out who would watch the children and where on earth we would get the money. I ran to Donovan and turned off *The Maury Povich Show* to make the announcement. He had the exact same questions but we both knew that there was no way we could miss this. We knew that reversal of established deficits was unlikely, but stopping progression in its tracks was the promised outcome, which apparently had happened for many ALS patients who traveled from all over North America to receive this treatment. We were lucky enough to be about an hour and a half away, and honestly, what were the chances of another cancellation?

Donovan's sister watched the boys, and I took cash out on our credit card, which made it slightly more than maxed out. I told Donovan that we would worry about paying it later, like when he was back at his job and could work some overtime.

Eeeeeek!

We arrived twenty minutes early and were surprised to find ourselves at an unassuming house on a residential street. The same lady that booked the appointment showed us into what looked like my nana's living room. I apologized for our early arrival and said that we were happy to wait. "The Doctor" was finishing up with a patient and would be with us momentarily. The decor appeared to be a power struggle between Christianity, 1972, and Bob Dylan. There were doilies over the arms of the velour settee, and a bible with several page markers on a table to our right with a large cross on the wall above it. Incense burned on the table to our left. A large, old-timey, framed picture of a man being baptized in a river hung on the wall.

The receptionist was kind enough to take our payment

while we waited so we could focus all of our energy on healing without distraction when the session ended.

A man slid open the frosted sliding glass doors dividing the waiting room and what was probably once a dining room that had been converted into a treatment room. He welcomed us with a massive smile, and mentioned that God welcomed us too. He was pleasant looking, around sixty years old, with grey hair pulled back in a long braid. He wore a white, button-down shirt with the sleeves rolled up and several top buttons undone, revealing thick grey chest hair that was tangled around a gold cross hanging from a chain.

"The Doctor" introduced himself and explained why his treatment was different from other healers with a similar practice. The key was his relationship with God. It was unique in that God spoke *directly* to him. This gave him the power, with God's help, to extract the negative energy that not only caused the disease but also prevented the healing. This essential step was something that only he and two others in the world could perform as it allowed the delivery of powerful, positive, healing energy.

Doctor/Healer: "Any questions before we start?"

Me: "Yes, why didn't the neurologist tell us about this?"

Doctor/Healer: "Well, you see, the pharmaceutical companies that fund the ALS clinic and the research it does make no money when God steps in."

Me: "Makes sense."

We chatted further about what to expect during the session and what would happen next. Donovan was asked about medical history, any medications, or allergies along with family history and dynamics.

Then they began. Donovan lay on a massage table with his shirt off. The Doctor tilted his head back and looked up, hovering his hands close to Donovan's body while moving them like he was giving him an imaginary bed bath. He then closed his eyes and nodded in agreement as he told the ceiling, "Yes, I feel it too." Excellent news . . . he is back with us. "The Lord and I have found the negative energy that is preventing your recovery. To release it, we must expose and confront the source. What trauma are you holding onto, my son? Was it a childhood event? Share it with me and find healing."

"I really didn't suffer any childhood trauma." Donovan was trying so hard to participate.

"Close your eyes; think hard. Remember yourself as a boy, eight or ten years old; what happened to make you so sad, so afraid? What is it you cannot talk about? Reveal it to me and let yourself be healed."

He sang/yelled the word *healed*. I was startled then managed to suppress a giggle at the pseudo sermon from this televangelist performance. I was sure he would eventually break character and begin the treatment we had paid for.

"I honestly had a happy childhood," Donovan was declaring. "My parents are still happily married and the only grandmother I have known is still with us."

The Doctor/Healer pressed on, asking over and over for Donovan to think harder, and reveal his hidden secret. Donovan finally broke his lifelong silence and admitted that the family dog died at some point when he was little; he couldn't quite remember the details. He was too young. The Doctor then raised a finger to quiet us and excused himself while he again conversed with the ceiling. He then told us that God was mistaken; the source of the negative energy was not childhood trauma. It was an addiction!

Nope.

It was a subverted, long-standing, covert lie!

Nope.

Finally, a breakthrough came when God once again amended his prediction because Donovan was fiercely independent, which made him a hard read.

There was a repressed memory that, along with his lust for watching violent hockey fights, caused the negativity that was keeping him sick.

Thanks a bunch, Tie Domi. (Domi was an enforcer for the Toronto Maple Leafs hockey team from 1994–2006. Fighter. Troublemaker. One of Donovan's heroes.)

Donovan was indeed a tough nut to crack, and for a minimal extra cost, a healing crystal known as a "reveal" was recommended to unearth the truth. However, until then, "No more hockey for you, young man. God's orders. God wants you to be flooded with peaceful images. No more violence."

The truth was that the truth had revealed itself long before God got all flustered and mixed up his energetic messages. The truth was very hard to swallow. We were desperate fools preyed on by a con man. We later found out that Julia's mother, along with beating ALS, was also winning the battle against colon cancer, and Alzheimer's, as well as not actually existing. We also learned that Julia had been escorted out of a cancer ward waiting room by security.

Rude.

She was just trying to share the gift of healing.

We hardly spoke as I drove us home. We were embarrassed, angry at the anal abscess of a person who took our money at a time when I washed my hair in dish soap and borrowed money for milk. And we were angry with ourselves for falling for it. But it wasn't the financial burden that was the most difficult aspect. It was the reality that we had to accept: there was no magic wand or hidden secret to healing.

There was no healing.

Donovan would return home physically the same, but we were not unchanged. We were poorer, and that was upsetting. We would forever be a little more cynical and a little less hopeful. We would never again have a conversation that widened my eyes, made me clap my hands and excitedly say, "Oh my God, but *what crash?*" A sad acceptance came home with us that day that eventually replaced the disappointment of our "un-healing" experience.

"We can grab the boys and still be home in time for

Hockey Night in Canada. Can I interest you in a bottle of beer with a creatively curly straw in it?"

"Beer is better through a straight straw."

"Done. Unfortunately, though, I must cover your eyes during the fights." Donovan laughed and then cried a bit. He watched all of the game, fights included, while sipping beer through a straight straw.

CHAPTER 9

Grief Pie

IN THAT PLACE THAT IS NOT QUITE ASLEEP and not quite awake, where dreams spill and swirl slowly into the light of morning; in that tiny moment that happens before the brain ignites, before reality makes itself known—that is where I wanted to stay that morning. I didn't want that moment to give way to the crash of my current existence, but crash it did. Landing on me, crushing my chest until all that was left to do was cry out. The sun had dared to cast dazzling beams through my blinds. I could see the dust moving and dancing while suspended and caught in a tractor beam as if this day were fine. I had, I thought, forbidden the sun from shining. With all my anger and tears, I had willed this day never to begin. Yet here it was, that defiant fucking morning. I buried my head in the covers and declined to participate. I would stay there and wallow in my misery. If the universe refused to stand still and mourn with me, then I would withdraw from it and exist only in my bed of abundant, snot-filled tissues.

Then I heard, "Dylan, you're such an idiot! Mum's going to kill you." Followed by, "You're not allowed to say *idiot*.

Mum's gonna kill YOU!" I threw back the duvet and reached for a clean tissue. Negotiating the peaceful resolution of this conflict would require an empty nose; also an empty bladder. I headed to the bathroom, resigning myself to the postponement of my personal defeat, which would have to be rescheduled to a more convenient time.

Today would be a funeral-shopping day. First the mall for appropriate funeral attire, followed by Costco for post-funeral snacks. Jonathan, senior-style adviser, was ready for the challenge of shopping on a budget. I suggested we start at the thrift shop, but that idea was quickly shot down. I thought it was completely reasonable to put the boys in gently used suits instead of spending large on suits that they would wear once before the new suits themselves would end up in the thrift shop. I was outvoted, and since my capacity to fight was greatly reduced, we headed to the mall.

Scouring the crowded lot for a place to park, Jonathan asked why no one in Canada was at work today. When I finally pulled into a spot, he said, "Good God, you may as well have left the car at home. You've parked bloody miles away." He then demanded to be carried. I offered to kick him in the shins instead. He then demanded that the boys carry him, and they took turns trying to lift him and pretend to piggyback him as they giggled their way through the parking lot. I smiled at the joy Jonathan brought when I simply could not. Our loss was every bit his loss, too, yet he never failed to bring us happiness. He had always been in tune with how the boys were feeling, ready with a well-timed inappropriate joke or impromptu wrestle. I cried as I watched him lift the weight of today's task from my boys. Throughout his stay with us, he had the ability to give them chunks of emotional respite instead of constantly wading through the swamp of sorrow that sucked the energy out of the grown-ups.

We headed to a discount men's clothing store that produced cheaply made suits with too much shine. Jonathan gingerly passed the material of a flashy suit draped over a mannequin through his fingers followed by a dramatic fake gag. Donovan-Rhys pulled at a metallic-looking blue-grey suit, but Jonathan suggested that something not made of foil would be more appropriate for this occasion. Dylan then declared that he had found "The One," but again, the all-white tux with red cummerbund and bow tie combo was not what I had in mind. Every boy-sized suit made them look like they were dressing up as James Bond for Halloween—that is, if Bond were underfed and dressed by Dumb and Dumber. We settled on plain trousers with a sports jacket. By this point in the shopping adventure, they would have agreed to wear bunny suits if it got them out of the store. Jonathan took them into the change room and they tried on their outfits.

They emerged from behind the curtain to pass the final inspection. Dylan had a big smile. "Mum, we look like defectives."

"Detectives," Donovan-Rhys corrected, emphasizing the absent *t* sound.

"Yes, you do, you gorgeous pair. I love that winning combination. Go and change and we'll pay." They disappeared behind the curtain in time for me to fold over and cry. My babies stood dressed in clothes for their dad's funeral. The gravity of it crippled me for a moment and I wrestled with that recurring wave of disbelief.

How could this be us?

There was a party planned to follow the funeral. Of course, it wasn't really a *party*, per se, but a wake or a "celebration of life." Friends kindly offered to chip in and make the food portion a potluck. The venue was moved from my tiny house to the Royal Canadian Legion. As the list of people planning to attend grew, and many of those people offered to bring food, there really wasn't much for us to prepare but it felt wrong not contributing to my own husband's funeral. I grabbed a Costco trolley on the way in and pushed it toward Jonathan and the kids who had made a beeline for the free samples. One wheel was wonky, spinning and squealing and only letting me turn left. Jonathan loudly pointed out my obvious misfortune. "The only thing worse than having the wonky wheel trolley is having it when shopping for your husband's funeral. It's like you entered the saddest human contest."

I was unfazed. He had already yelled across the store that he had found the Costco-sized tube of Preparation H for me. We gathered our shareables and I took the pair of beginner scuba diving sets out of the cart and replaced them with the promise of French fries on the way out. We divided and conquered the rest of the trip. Jonathan and Dyl went for fries; I stood with the cart in the checkout queue and listened in as Donovan-Rhys, always the social butterfly, chatted to the lady in the line next to us.

Donovan-Rhys: "Oh, I wanted an apple pie like you but Mum said no."

Lady just wanting to peacefully pay for her groceries: "Well, I only have one because of a special occasion. It's my husband's birthday tomorrow and apple pie is his favorite."

Donovan-Rhys: "It's my favorite too. I hope he has a happy birthday. We have a special occasion too. My daddy died and we are funeral shopping. Mum says that apple pie isn't shareable funeral food, and also, she's not made of money."

I choked on my take-out coffee while hoping for an earthquake or robbery to spice up this moment. I forced a smile and mouthed a "sorry" to the mortified lady, and Donovan-Rhys provided her with the unsolicited help of loading her shopping onto the belt while she blinked back tears, checking her bag for an imaginary *anything*. She paid and left in that hurried, "I don't know how to respond to death or grief" sort of way.

No one does.

Don't beat yourself up. Even once we've experienced loss, we still don't know what to do when we are faced with it or how to be around it. Although, undoubtedly, some responses are worse than others.

Things people *actually* said to me following my husband's death:

- "You'll be okay after a while. Time heals all things."
- "I understand how you feel. I put my cat down last summer."

- "You shouldn't feel too sad; you knew it was coming."
- "At least he's in a better place; his suffering is over."
- "At least you're young."
- "The kids are so young, they might be able to forget him."
- "At least you knew he was going to die."
- "At least you had time to prepare."
- "What will you do with all that spare time now?"

All of these clumsy attempts at comfort came from well- meaning people. They were accompanied by the head tilt/arm rub while the well-meaner punched me in the gob with their bungling words of pity. They didn't intend to be hurtful, but pity is useless and can do nothing but cause injury. It is an attempt at compassion that lacks commitment, which makes it a spectator sport serving only the one who pities. It is solely for the ones who gain momentary satisfaction that they have participated in grief. Thankfully, many people were able to refrain from pity; they didn't try to fix the situation or offer advice. Some were just plain honest. A wonderful friend left the following note:

Dear Hayley, Donovan-Rhys and Dylan,
*   I don't know what the right thing to say is.*
*   I do know that you really don't want to be at the grocery store right now.*
*   I am thinking of you all.*
*   Love Annette.*

The note was left on my doorstep attached to several bags of grocery essentials.

We collected our fries and limped our broken buggy to the exit. (I feel you, broken buggy.) Just outside of the *Have you paid?* checkpoint, we were stopped by the lady Donovan-Rhys had traumatized in the checkout line. She said, "Your son had such an honest conversation with me. I did not expect that my Costco visit would include a lesson from a little boy that will stay with me forever. I am sorry for what you're going through. Would I be stepping on toes if I thanked your son with an apple pie?"

I took a second to process this stranger's gentle kindness, her commitment to compassion, before answering, "That would be really thoughtful. Thank you."

Donovan-Rhys was delighted and also triumphant in a sort of snotty way that made me want to trip him as he used both hands and forearms to carry his colossal pie through the parking lot.

(Calm down. I obviously didn't. It was too public.)

As we walked away, Jonathan asked what all that was about and I explained about the checkout interaction between Donovan-Rhys and the lady. He then said to Donovan-Rhys, "Oh my God, Donovan-Rhys, you lucky thing! Next time, request a PlayStation instead of an apple pie though."

CHAPTER 10

I "Sister" You

MY SISTER, AND ONLY SIBLING, is almost eight years younger than me. She was born with a mop of jet-black curls and huge blue eyes. One of her irises had a striking hazel birthmark and her skin was milky white and flawless. In comparison, I was a heavy, clumsy, redheaded child with freckles and a frown. People would stop us on the street to marvel at my sister's beauty. When they'd ask her name, I would offer up, "Owen-Rhys," which would have been her name if she were a boy. My mother would laugh, introduce "Kate," and point out the touch of jealousy I was experiencing. Old ladies would peer into her pram and gasp at her beauty, calling her a porcelain doll, and tell me how lucky I was. Why the hell was I lucky? Lady, you should get a kick in the shins.

Upon her arrival, my once solitary living space was immediately filled with the sound of crying—and rife with the bouquet of baby poo. The number of requests to fetch and carry went through the roof, and I was forced to interact with this creature by taking her for walks to the park or around our neighborhood. My mother would hear me open the front door after bumping the pram backward up the stone steps of our terraced house and proceed to shout from the living room that I hadn't been gone long enough. She'd inevitably send us back out for another lap.

As a toddler, my sister helped herself to my collection of pristine, unboxed, foreign dolls. The dolls hailed from a variety of worldly locales and were gifted to me by neighbors who traveled far and wide. They all sported the colorful, traditional dress representing their country of origin. The dolls fed my imagination with all the places I would visit someday, as an unshackled adult. Much to my chagrin, my sister decided to unbox them, undress them, and cut the hair of several of my poor dolls. I would come home from school and discover the carnage, demanding to know why the devil's spawn was left unsupervised.

I'd then be told, "She's just a baby. She doesn't understand."

I ran away from home once. I'm not sure if it was because of my sister, but it does seem reasonable to blame her at this point. I packed my red Cindy doll vanity case with half a loaf of bread and grabbed my headless Louby Lou doll for company, then headed out of the house before anyone was awake. In case you're wondering, Louby Lou was a fabric rag dog that stood as tall as me. She used to have a head with a plastic face, but my parents had a fight wherein Louby was used as a makeshift weapon. My mum swung her by her stripy legs and cracked her face on some part of my father. Her face split into two pieces, stuffing spilling through the gap where her nose should be. It was suggested that she be thrown away, but my objections were noted and we compromised. Mum removed her head and sewed the neck hole shut.

I should mention that I did not grow up in a violent home. Though, admittedly, my dad, a career police officer, did have a shocking temper. He frequently threw teapots up the back garden when they dared to miss the cup, hurled for causing tea to drip on the counter. And I once saw him beat up a vacuum cleaner. But the only person I ever saw him smack was my sister when she was a toddler. (OK, small lie; I did see him hit an archenemy of the local police who we encountered in town. Dad and I were driving in the opposite direction of this person when he shouted an obscene and unrepeatable insult all the way across the road at my dad. Dad turned the car around and drove two wheels up onto the curb to be within arm's reach. He then grabbed the man by his dirty shirt, punched him on the nose, and advised him not to be rude before we drove off. I'm not sure if I'm allowed to tell that story, so under your hat, please.)

Anyway, back to my sister's brief encounter with corporal punishment. Dad told my sister that he would spank her if her naughty behavior continued. So, with hands on hips, Kate decided to poke out her tongue—and he proceeded to give her a smack on her bum.

Kate retorted with, "That didn't hurt."

I believe she was right, and I am quite sure that it hurt

Dad more than it did her. That was the end of smacks from Dad. He was—and still is—a wonderful father, but he was not always a good husband. On very rare occasions, Mum would snap and throw (or swing) something in his general direction—usually with little to no injury. As the history of my parents' marriage was revealed to me in early adulthood, I understood how patient, kind, and forgiving my mother was. I should probably be sending her flowers far more often—even though she once stood on my foot so I couldn't run away, then smacked me with the pipe of the vacuum cleaner. We are talking about the eighties here ... but that sucker was metal.

As a chubby runaway, actual running was out of the question. So I headed to the bus stop. I understood that there would be some kind of interaction that occurred with the driver; I'd seen my mother do it on plenty of occasions. So when the bus arrived, I climbed aboard like a boss.

"Nana Redman's house, please. Number 42, Llanfach Road."

"Going on your own, are you?"

"Yes, I'm running away."

"Oh, right, then. You'd better take a seat, my lovely." Louby Lou and I were the only people on the bus. I thought nothing of it when the bus pulled up right at Nana's gate instead of the designated stop; I just hopped down the steps and said, "Thanks, Drive."

What had actually happened, I subsequently learned, was that the bus driver recognized the family name as well as the oddness of an unattended, runaway little girl and put his bus out of service to make sure I stayed safe and got to my destination. He then reported the situation—and word got back to Dad. It was bound to happen, but I was already under Nana Redman's wing so I was basically untouchable. She was more mortified that I had made the journey in public with a headless doll than concerned about my potential abduction. She punished me by making me a doorstep of toast from freshly delivered crusty bread, spread with beef drippings from a roast she had cooked the night before, and sprinkled salt on top. I then picked peas from the garden with Grampa Redman, and we sat on the floor in front of the coal fireplace with a basket of them to shell, putting the empties in one pot and the shelled peas in another. I'd sneak perfectly emptied shells back in with the full ones to try and trick Grampa. He would pick up the empty shell without looking then gasp and roll back with shock at the impostor, every single time. I would climb on his lap and demand a story accounting for every one of the blue scars that his hands were covered in. They came from a lifetime of working far belowground in a South Wales coal mine, but he told me tales of wrestling dragons—probably because he was the greatest human who ever lived.

My dad did the same for my boys. In their short, transatlantic visits, Grampy Wales forged the type of relationship that only grandpas can. Tickly monster, storyteller, ball thrower, and swing-pusher. Regular stuff. But in my house, for my boys, it was so much more. It was the thoughtful and gentle replacement of a father's actions while still making his terminally ill son-in-law feel loved and included. Genius, right? I am not sure how he managed to find the right balance. I am sure that he is the only man, ever, in my boys' lives to provide the same, unshakeable, consistent, reliable love, before and after their dad died. Even through those distant, late teenage years, Donovan-Rhys and Dylan would never doubt the ability to reach out and know that Grampy Wales was there for them. How we underestimate the tenderness and utter necessity of a grandparent's love.

Kate was annoying in the way sisters were supposed to be. She would place several cups upside down on the stairs and tell me that there was a spider caught under one of them. In Wales, we had house spiders the size of dinner plates, so I was left trapped on the second floor until I could pay some unreasonable fee or be rescued by a parent. She would frequently march into the house to tattle on me, shouting, "HAYLEY HIT ME BACK!" And she was *always* in my room when she shouldn't be.

I left home for Canada at Kate's most impressionable age; it was like leaving a piece of myself. I missed a great deal of the things a sister should be there for; she navigated the demise of our parents' marriage alone, without me even knowing about it. She went through a host of teenage turmoil while I was oblivious to anything going on outside of my own, all-consuming home life. She grew up.

Despite the distance, we managed to stay connected. She would travel from Wales and spend every summer with

Donovan and me. She was about eleven years old when she and Donovan first met. He treated her both like a princess and as one of the guys. Over the years, he taught her how to box and throw a proper punch, refining form and stance as they did a boxer's dance around the living room. She put her skill into practice when she was back home and my dad gave her a gentle teasing finger tap on the chin and then bobbed and weaved around her, enticing her to play. Instead of pounding at him with flailing, easy-to-miss, wide swings, she tucked her chin and brought her forearms up to elevens before sending an explosive right-hand jab at him. My dad grabbed his bicep and stood back in shock, asking where on earth she had learned that.

"My big brother taught me how to box. Don't mess with me, Dad."

Donovan also taught her the ins and outs of hockey and to love the Toronto Maple Leafs. She worshipped him—and their bond became immediately unbreakable. The more she visited Canada, the more accustomed to the way of life she became. (With the possible exception of that time she took a phone call from the marketing division of a lawn care company. I listened to her side of the conversation.)

"No. Really? Oh my God! No, thank you!" She hung up the phone. "You won't believe this. That was the *weed* man! He wants to drop off *a sample* at the house! I am shocked. I have to go to the pub for mine."

Kate loved being with us and, like I did, fell in love with Canada. I don't know if she could fully grasp the gravity of Donovan's diagnosis at a young age, and there never seemed to be a moment when the weight of what was happening caught up with her. She just adapted. Visit after visit she accepted and loved the new version of Donovan. Each visit, she loved her nephews a little more and made her mark as their favorite aunty, spoiling them, showering them with affection and always ready to undermine any discipline I doled out. As she got older, her personality and wit taught my husband humility and grounding that I could not. He tolerated her sassy sarcasm more than he did mine, and she would never hold back. While the rest of the world made concessions for Donovan in every way, Kate did not. She called him out on his behavior and his bullshit. She made fun of him, actually. I should say that *she made fun of everyone*, and he was not spared.

"Are you on an ask-a-thon? Six times my sister has tried to sit and eat," she would scold him, and he would laugh.

"Last thing. I promise."

He would ask her to reach for his drink, and as she was doing so she would add, "Oh my God. Lazy! That's what you are." Then he would laugh and snort and be unable to drink from the straw she was offering him.

The banter only increased when our cousin Jonathan was added to the mix. As an older teenager, he visited almost as much as Kate. They grew up together in Wales, living down the street from each other. They were extremely close and a sarcastic force to be reckoned with. They were unapologetically inappropriate, usually at a time when it was most needed or most embarrassing. Their visits were a breath of fresh air to me. They entertained the boys, helped with

Donovan, and were such good company. (Except for that one time when they took advantage of their freedom and got drunk on rum and peach Snapple. Jonathan got lost on his way to the bathroom and vomited over a shelf of toys, flooding Hot Wheels cars and the Fisher-Price school bus with foul-smelling goo. My sister did not even attempt to get to the bathroom. She vomited where she slept then laid her face back down in it. I made these grizzly discoveries about twenty minutes before my first day care child was due to arrive. In the middle of my yelling at the pair of them, my sister peeled her face from her bed to reach down and grab an open Diet Coke bottle. She tipped the bottle up to her pukey mouth, took a swig, then offered it to Jonathan. Shockingly, he declined.)

Mostly, the summer visits were filled with good memories, amazing recollections, and laughter. One evening, Kate sat Donovan into his chair to feed him dinner, but he was immediately uncomfortable. He rocked his body and tried to get out the words to explain his situation as my sister stood next to him and suggested, "Why don't you sit still for a sec so you can tell me what is wrong?" He followed the advice, took a breath, and managed to say, "Move the pillow."

He was half-sitting on a decorative pillow that was the source of the discomfort. Kate pulled out the offending pillow and began feeding Donovan dinner.

While noting the exaggerated amount of drama over

the pillow, Jonathan sipped his tea and casually offered up, "There is nothing worse than sitting on a scratchy pillow though. Not even famine in Africa." This started an uncontrollable giggling fit from Donovan that would spontaneously reemerge over the next several days.

People with ALS can be prone to exaggerated emotional responses; uncontrollable laughing or crying is common. With Kate and Jonathan in the house, laughter was guaranteed.

As the years passed and Donovan deteriorated, the humor, sarcasm, and banter remained unrelenting. The subtle changes that did occur in my sister and cousin crept in as slowly and surely as the disease did for Donovan. Added to the silliness was the ability to adapt as two young adults learned how to care for a dying man. There were no "how to" lessons; they were never taught anything. They simply embraced the necessity to adjust and did so with no change to how they felt or acted toward Donovan. Little by little, they added to their portfolio of caregiving skills. Feeding the right amount, at the right pace. Lifting and transferring Donovan to a wheelchair. Wiping his face with a warm, damp cloth with exactly the right amount of pressure. Giving of themselves while always hiding their sadness behind a cast-iron barrier of humor.

Following a particularly severe but well-deserved ribbing, Donovan once suggested that the two of them give him a break.

"How about you lay off? I am the one with a terminal illness, y'know?"

They immediately, without exchanging words, started looking for something. Lifting cushions, moving curtains . . .

"You asked for this one," I warned, knowing what was coming.

"What are you looking for?" Donovan dared to ask.

"Oh . . . your *exemption*! It's gotta be around here somewhere. The pass that makes you more special than the rest of us; you know, the anti-teasing pass."

Jonathan's eyes lit up as he reached into his pocket. "Found it!" he announced. "I think this belongs to you." He pulled his fist out of his pocket with the middle finger fully extended and offered it to Donovan. They then fell about laughing, as I shook my head and asked Donovan why he would even try to take them on.

Damn amateur.

For Donovan, being treated the same as everyone else was something he strived for. He was intelligent and strong-minded and wanted to be recognized. To be spoken *with*, not over. He could answer his own questions. He hated that sitting in a wheelchair made him invisible or dismissible to some. Kate and Jonathan never saw him as disabled or diseased. They saw the man who was an important part of their young lives and treated him the same no matter his deterioration. It was a treatment that Donovan could trust. He didn't always love the sarcasm, but he did love the honesty and consistency. He trusted them both with his intimate vulnerabilities, and they became familiar with his needs, which only strengthened their bond. Jonathan was his brother just as much as Kate was his sister.

When the summers ended, I would ban all talk of leaving or going home to Wales until the last possible moment. I wouldn't help pack (which would account for the leaving of many mismatched socks and countless clothing items), and all mention of flights and check-ins was avoided. When it was time to drive them to the airport, I would go and sit in the car to avoid witnessing the goodbyes taking place in the house. When the time came, I never concealed my sadness to see them go, but I never expressed or even truly understood the impact of their departure. It was more than missing a loved one. It was missing the camaraderie; missing having someone in my corner. It was also the end of a respite when I could share my load, share my laughs, and indulge in a little bit of back home. I would hold on to them for just a little bit too long before letting them disappear through security, knowing that adult hugs were as few and far between as the visitors that brought them.

"I sister you" was a sentiment that I "stole" from a podcast. The host was talking about the bond between sisters and explaining that *I love you* is simply inadequate to express the lifetime of love that sisters share.

I wholeheartedly agree.

CHAPTER 11

The Funeral

THERE WAS A WEEK between Donovan's death and his funeral. It was somewhat like the week between Christmas and New Year's, a no-man's-land where no one is quite sure of what day it is and it doesn't really matter. It was a week filled with the maximum of everything—visitors, condolences, funeral planning, funeral shopping, food drop-offs, and emotions that ran at a ten out of ten. The week reached its climactic finale on funeral day, then, after a huge event-concluding fireworks display, everyone returned to their real lives.

I had thought about Donovan's funeral. Donovan had not. Or, if he had, I wasn't privy to those thoughts. He was never really open to talking about the end; he spent most of his illness denying it would come, and when denial was no longer an option, when the end was a clearly laid path, his emotions were fragile and conversations around the subject were quickly redirected. He had once made mention of having the band Blue Rodeo play live at his funeral, which would be at a pub, while the girls from Hooters served drinks from an open bar. Presumably, I was paying for the open bar, the band, and the waitstaff. In an uncharacteristically harsh move, I told him that none of that would be happening.

With no other direction and no experience in the funeral planning department, I went with a more traditional event. I wanted to do every part of it right. I felt the perceived judgment of the world saying, "Oh my God, she had *years* to get this right and *this* is what she came up with?" I had already fucked up the cremation. Not the actual cremation of Donovan's body—that was successful. But the part where I forgot to take socks to the funeral home and, more importantly, the part where I had him cremated before his entire family could visit with his body. Cremation was one of the only things Donovan had been clear on. What I didn't know was that there was a certain amount of time that should be allotted for visiting before letting the funeral home take the loved one away. I still don't understand the exact rules on this. If someone could please drop me a line and let me know the ins and outs of death etiquette, I would appreciate it. So, on top of my husband dying, my sister-in-law was angry with me for robbing her of a final goodbye. The other in-laws were also angry that I had made their sister/daughter even more upset on the day her brother died. So, yeah, I had to get the next bit right.

I had imagined a cloud-filled sky with a soft drizzle, a somber day punctuated with methodical movements throughout because slowing it all down and being deliberate was the key to conveying proper respect. As with many things in life, expectation and reality were far removed from each other. The morning of the funeral was sunny and unseasonably warm. The house was noisy with shouts of who was next in line to use the only tiny bathroom. Both of my parents were there, along with my sister and my cousin Jonathan—and of course Donovan-Rhys and Dylan. The kettle was always on, there was a constant shortage of tea mugs, and at all times, at least one person was looking for something they had just laid down. Dylan declared that he would be wearing a Batman shirt to the funeral, complete with a cape stitched to the shoulders, and I couldn't find my hairbrush. That morning, surrounded by everyone I loved, moving through a swirl of glorious, bustling chaos, was almost perfect. If only it weren't the day of my husband's funeral.

Over the years, while driving through our little town in his wheelchair, Donovan had developed a sort of celebrity status. He had befriended many of the residents and left an impression on everyone he met. So many people wanted to say goodbye.

A few days prior, the funeral home had announced that they did not have sufficient space for us and asked that we move the proceedings to St. James Anglican Church. Once more, this didn't fit with how I thought things would go. However, the move was definitely necessary. This was in part because of the crowd expected, and partly because my dad could not be contained. Back at home, my dad was a rugby player who also sang in the Welsh Male Voice Choir. His choir and Welsh rugby team had visited Canada when on tour and sang with the Welsh Male Voice Choir in Burlington, Ontario, and played several matches with the Centaurs rugby team. These were separate events, of course, but the people who played rugby were the same people who sang in the choir. (Singing and rugby go hand in hand. Not sure why; might be the booze.) His travels made him some lifelong Canadian friends who rallied when they heard of Donovan's death. The Burlington Male Voice Choir would be performing and leading the hymns at his funeral, and only an old and beautiful, acoustically perfect church would do.

Eventually, we all managed to get a turn in the bathroom. Dad, characteristically, waited until the rest of us were putting on shoes before jumping in the shower. He'd say, "Love, we'll *make* time," every time he was told there was no time for whatever was causing the delay. Then, all of a sudden, we were ready. Dressed. Made up and gathered at the door. The absence of chaos was an unfilled void. It was an oversight; I had packed every moment with distraction and had no time to really see my most loved people.

I became acutely aware of the missing piece.

The house would be empty for the first time in a very long time; yet, exiting was a matter of walking out. There was no wrestling with a wheelchair, remembering equipment or medications. My seven- and nine-year-old boys wore matching suits; we were all dressed up. Despite a week of planning, as I looked us over, it finally occurred to me that we were going to my husband's funeral.

A great many friends of Donovan had made offers to perform readings, dedications, and expressed their wish to share memories. There were so many requests that some of the sharing had to wait until the reception. Our very good friend and professional singer Jonie performed a beautiful and moving solo of "For the Beauty of the Earth" and did so with unwavering grace. My dad spoke and also shared Clare Harner's poem "Immortality." Reminding us that death is a transformation, not finality. Donovan's dad bravely spoke about the strength of his son, and as I watched a father speak at his child's funeral, it was clear to me where that strength came from. Donovan-Rhys wrote a poem of his own, which his uncle helped him read aloud. In case you missed the gravity here—my nine-year-old son read a poem that he wrote on his own, aloud, at his dad's funeral.

The Greatest Dad Who Had ALS

When my dad was young
He used to be a boxer.
He won lots of times and
Knocked people out.
He got lots of medals and
Won every bout.
When my dad was a man
He got ALS.
He couldn't walk or play
But we had fun every day.
Movies, jokes, and wheelchair rides
And so much love it touched the sky.
Now he's gone to heaven
To be with baby Jesus and Nana.
I miss him so much
That I don't know what to do
And I don't know what to think.
I'll just keep my special memories
In my heart and love him every day.

—Donovan-Rhys, aged nine

Almost everything about the funeral was well planned; I took some comfort in having control over the day's events—or so I thought. What I didn't know was that my closest friends had arranged something a little extra. One of the most moving things I have ever witnessed was seeing them take their seats in the church to say goodbye to their friend, all wearing Toronto Maple Leafs hockey jerseys with Donovan's name across their shoulders. Five families, children included, wearing a uniform that truly honored Donovan. If you only knew one thing about Donovan, it would be that he was the biggest fan of the Toronto Maple Leafs. This gesture was the greatest summary of the years of love they had already given us both. As they stood together, a weeping misfit hockey team, the *Hockey Night in Canada* theme song played to introduce a slideshow of Donovan's life that would conclude the service. A Garth Brooks song played as Donovan's life was reflected in photographs: *Life is better left to chance. I could have missed the pain but I'd have had to miss the dance.* The music played and the tears flowed. I looked around the overcrowded church at the lives Donovan had touched. I looked at my boys and would have given my own life at that very moment to spare their confusion, sadness, and pain. I wondered how I had arrived at this point—*and whose life was this, anyway?*

The funeral day ended. (I would tell you about the reception but I got drunk and only remember being back at home where my friend Kim and I raced to the bathroom. She shoved me out of the way and sat on the toilet. I was busting, too, so I sat on the edge of the bath and peed next to her.) I suspected it would but its enormity made me wonder what would happen next. Surely, life would not simply continue. Surely, people wouldn't start going about their business as if nothing had happened. And what of my life? I had already noticed the space grow. It's the space that used to be filled with the needs of a dying man. I thought I didn't have enough hours in the day. I thought I was the busiest person on the planet—but I had already noticed the space. Even in the weird week between the death and the funeral, that busy week where the mind is occupied with planning and visitors and saying "as well as can be expected, y'know," I noticed. I noticed the pull of distraction. It's the urge to keep moving for no reason. To fill time and never be unoccupied. Never—I mean ever—stop long enough to let your mind begin to contemplate what you've been through.

I had moved back into my own bedroom. Donovan and I moved into the family room months before to facilitate more equipment and ease of care. Before that, we were in our own room; Donovan in his hospital bed and me in Donovan-Rhys's single bed, while Donovan-Rhys slept in our queen-sized bed in his room.

For the first time in many years, I was back in my own room, in my own bed. I noticed Donovan-Rhys had scraped "I hat you" into the pine headboard, following some unjust removal of electronics time as a punishment for an infraction I can no longer recall. I was back in my bed but not alone; I was with my sister. I had slept alone in a single bed for years with literally no human contact, and yet I found myself unable to be alone in my own bed. So my sister slept with me. She would slide a sleepy hand onto my shoulder to comfort me when she heard me sobbing in the night. The weight of her arm reminded me of how it felt to be cared for. For years I had done all of the caring and comforting. I had been the giver of the soothing head rub and gentle hugs. I had done the wrestling it took to lift a grown man out of bed, and yes, I had done the bum-wiping. Her comfort made me cry with more intensity, but only because I had missed it so much.

Only one day after the funeral, I was forced to go to the grocery store. We could live off a freezer full of grief casserole for quite some time, but we no longer had milk for our tea. The crisis had to be dealt with. I felt irrationally terrified of bumping into someone I knew and having to fake my "okayness" so they would feel more okay. I bent my neck to look into each aisle before venturing down, making sure that the coast was clear. Not surprisingly, I saw someone I knew. What was surprising? They were laughing and chatting with someone they knew. I felt a lump rise in my throat and tears threatened my eyes with their stingers. These so-called semi-acquaintance "friends" were acting like this was a normal fucking day. Had they forgotten? Were they ignorant to the sorrow with which the world was engaged? How dare they! I spun my cart around to turn my back on this appalling behavior, uncertain if I could even finish the task at hand. *Pull yourself together, girl*, I told myself. *You have no control over the arseholes of the world but currently control your family's tea-drinking ability*. I grabbed the milk and added it to the cart and didn't look up again until I was in the queue to pay. The cashier I always go to was talking to the customer ahead of me as I was placing groceries on the conveyor belt.

Holy shit! Those bitches were talking about how nice the weather was for October and what a beautiful day it was! When it was my turn, the cashier recognized me and tilted her head to the side before saying, "I am so sorry to hear about your husband. How are you coping?"

So I leaned over and grabbed a fist full of her nasty oversprayed hair and pulled her toward me while screaming, "What the fuck do you care? You were enjoying the lovely sunshine one second ago!" Not really; I smiled and said, "You know, as well as can be expected, I suppose."

"Well, you go and take care of those little boys; they are what matters now."

I was shocked. It's the boys that I should take care of now? A revelation.

So I said, "They are? I had no fucking idea. Shit, I should never have left them at home alone, in the bath, while playing with power tools. Thanks, Sandra, you're a bloody genius."

Not really. I smiled and said, "Thanks, Sandra. That's very kind of you."

In one small trip to the grocery store, I learned that the world and the majority of people in it didn't miss a beat. It was business as usual for most, back to business as usual for the rest, and complete turmoil and devastation for the rest of the rest.

How long it takes to climb out of that pit of turmoil and start working on business as usual depends on how far into the hole you have fallen. For some, there is no climbing out. Business will never be usual because things cannot ever be the same. Instead, eventually, a new usual will emerge, a new way to look and move forward. There might even be a way to understand that the only person capable of feeling and carrying the grief of losing a spouse is another grieving spouse.

I have never suffered the loss of a parent. I could only try to love my boys enough for both my husband and myself, but I didn't know their particular loss. Thankfully, I have never lost a child—and my God, that must carry a singular, more unimaginable sort of pain. But I guess what I learned, or started to learn while at the store, was that pain, grief, loss, and our response to it are very personal. If the worst loss you have suffered is that of your grandparent, then that is your ten. Your ten is as poignant to you as mine is to me and it is not a competition of who can hurt the most. Even the most empathetic person was going to go ahead and appreciate the sunshine when all I could see was darkness. At that moment, in that store, I began to realize that attempting to see the sunshine—or at least accepting that it exists instead of being angry and inhabiting the depths of darkness—might be my way forward. Forward movement can happen and should happen at an individual pace. The loss of a person, whether it is a husband, parent, child, or friend, is permanent. I understand how obvious this is, but the pressure to pull ourselves together, move on, and make it so other people are less uncomfortable with our grief causes us to rush to recover.

Go ahead, rush. Skip steps. Recover on someone else's timeline. Grief is patient, but it is not kind. It will wait for a while, but eventually you will participate.

You will grieve.

Donovan would be dead for the rest of my life. There was no value in rushing to reach imaginary grief recovery milestones on anyone else's time frame but my own. I tried accepting that other people's ability to move forward, to move on and see the sunshine, was not a personal attack. Sometimes I was successful. As Rebecca Yarros said, "Grief had no mercy, time limit, or expiration date."

CHAPTER 12

We All Fall Down

I am swimming toward the surface. Light is dancing across the gentle movement of water. Glints of sunlight bounce from each tiny wave, playfully, without care—basking in their freedom. I see the joy, but it cannot penetrate these depths. I rhythmically kick, a consistent upward effort, but the distance remains. The darkness tells me about its comfort and reminds me of the effort required to reach the warmth. We both acknowledge that the attempt is tiring. The darkness prevails at exploitation with little coercion. After all, it doesn't seem so bad down here; I think I'll stay awhile.

First, there were fasciculations, or rapid and prolonged muscle twitches. They were not painful, but they would drive Donovan crazy. Once further signs of disease progression emerged, the fasciculations were allotted less attention. One of the earlier deficits noted was something the clinic called drop foot. The anterior muscles of the lower leg are responsible for dorsiflexion or bringing the toes back up so the heel hits the ground first, when walking. Weakness in those muscles causes drop foot. Sometimes the toes would catch on the ground and Donovan would trip. He tried to be thoughtful and safe about every step, but inevitably, the falls happened. In the beginning, for the most part, this occurred in the yard when he was walking over an uneven surface, such as our lawn. Like a slow-motion toddler, his toe would catch the grass and he would crumple to the ground. I would silently pray to whoever was in charge of inappropriate reactions to help me stop laughing before he looked up and saw my face.

"Are you hurt?" I would shout while deep breathing through fits of silent laughter and staying out of the line of sight until I could get a grip. *What on earth is wrong with me? Why is the sight of someone falling so funny?*

"I know you're laughing; just come and help me up." I would tug him into a sitting position and mouth "sorry." We would spend a minute sitting on the grass together, him doing a body scan for injuries. Me trying to compose my giggling self.

"You'd laugh if your granny's arse was on fire," he'd say. "Good thing it's just whiplash and a traumatic brain injury."

"Would not!" I objected. "I'm not a monster." Although my nana Redman, to the best of my knowledge, never caught her arse on fire, she did catch her white, wispy hair on fire once. She bent over to check the oven and while doing so put her head too close to the lit gas burner. She then asked if I could smell something burning. I was laughing so hard; I almost couldn't get the words out. It only got worse when she started beating herself with a tea towel. My uncle Alan came into the kitchen to investigate the commotion; he was familiar with the scene, and upon seeing my nana's singed hair, said, "Caught your hair on fire again, did you, Mam?" So, I concede, I do have a history of inappropriate laughing. Once I incongruously and inexplicably laughed at a funeral. It was my aunt's funeral. My aunt Janice, who sat in the pew behind me, rubbed my shaking shoulders and said, "There, there," in an attempt to console me.

Oh my God. Maybe I am a monster!

If that is the case, I fully blame my dad for demanding that the laughter stop because *the dinner table was no place for that nonsense.* If there is one way to reinforce inappropriate laughter, it is to insist that the offending person chuckling should immediately halt their transgression. How does that work? My sister and I would then exchange knowing looks and, subsequently, milk would be expelled with a robust force from our noses.

The first medical device we were introduced to was a simple, rigid, molded plastic splint that went under Donovan's foot and up the back of his leg fastened with Velcro strapped around his calf, thus preventing the foot from dropping. He walked like a robot, but it worked well as long as he was wearing sturdy shoes. My mum sewed a non-slip backing to Donovan's slippers to help prevent falls in the house (and polishing the floor with wax was a strict no-no). Mum would walk backwards, in front of him, when he moved around the house, ready to steady his balance at any moment. Obviously, one person walking backwards leading another with poor balance was a clear sign that the dog should immediately get underfoot. I would often hear a stumble and my mother then shout, "Scruff, you little bastard." Which would make me giggle once more.

Not all falls were funny. All falls required a rapid severity assessment and only those deemed minor would move on to the hilarity assessment, over which I had no control. As falls became more frequent, the laughter became less so. On the day that Kylee was due to fly back to British Columbia following a summer visit, Donovan had a fall. She was traveling as an unaccompanied minor and would be escorted from airport drop-off by an airline attendant until her mother met her on the other side. I drove us to the airport, parked in the disabled parking area, and unfolded Donovan's wheelchair from the boot. We headed into the departures terminal. All checked in, we made our way to security to say our goodbyes. Kylee, with her "Unaccompanied Minor" lanyard, was ushered to a separate area of the security check where she would meet her escort. Except that was not to be. Her parent or guardian, we were now informed, had to be cleared by security and take Kylee to the departure gate; she would meet her escort there. Okey dokey, no problem. Let's go. However, *only* her parent or guardian was authorized to take her through. No one else.

"And that is Mr. Donovan." The security man read the document we had just given him.

"So, I can't go through?" I looked for clarification.

"No," retorted security man.

"Will someone from security take him through so he can take her through?"

"No."

"It will be someone from the airline?" Could no one see the issue here?

"No."

"Then could you please tell me how my husband is supposed to escort his daughter to the departure gate? Who will push his wheelchair?" This may have had a slightly irritated tone.

"Ma'am. It is not my job to solve your problems. It is only to inform you of the rules and enforce them."

"Oh my God. Am I on camera here? This is the most fu—"

Donovan interrupted me as I was about to take on airport security—which, by the way, I could have done with ease if this dimwit was their standard.

"Help me up." Donovan was already shifting his weight forward in his chair. "I'll walk her there. If we waste any more time arguing, she will miss her flight."

"No. It's too far. This is ridiculous." I was already helping him. He found his balance and was wearing his leg braces. I hugged Kylee and watched the pair of them walk away. Kylee pulled her suitcase and helped her dad walk, Donovan swaying with the awkward gait that is common for people with ALS.

Too much time had passed and there was not one thing I could do. I asked various staff members if they could check the route to the gate, but not one of them could. Kylee's flight was in the air before I saw Donovan again. After saying goodbye to his daughter, Donovan started walking back; he guessed that he had made it about halfway before catching a piece of carpet with his toe and falling forward, trapping his arms beneath him and getting a rug burn on his cheekbone. After substantial effort, he managed to build enough momentum to flip himself onto his side so he could try and get the attention of the people walking by him. His voice and speech were weak because of ALS. That weakness was exacerbated by the workout he had just put himself through. He was unable to call out so he watched as people walked around him. Passengers, various airline staff, and airport personnel. At one point, the person who drives the shuttle for people who need assistance getting to their flights honked his horn and informed Donovan that he could not lie down there. Finally, he caught the eye of a lady walking past, a passenger, trying to get to her flight. She stood her wheelie case upright and asked if he needed help. He couldn't make a sound come out, but nodded his head and cried with relief. She crouched next to him and asked if she could help sit him up and lean him against the wall. He nodded and she pulled his body toward her until he was sitting.

"That looks a little better." She stood back and admired her handiwork before dragging her case away. She returned a few minutes later with two airport staff and a wheelchair. She gave them instructions on how to lift Donovan from the floor and into the chair. She then took a tissue from her bag and cleaned Donovan's carpet-burned face, some from the initial fall, some from trying to push himself up. He was half expecting her to spit on the tissue to get a proper, motherly clean, but she didn't. Clearly, this lady either had experience in the medical field or dealing with special needs—or perhaps she just had some human decency. She asked if he needed anything else, taking one of his hands in both of hers and apologizing for having to leave; boarding was being called at her gate. Donovan, having caught his breath, was able to say "Thank you" and clumsily plopped his free hand onto hers.

The airport staff brought my husband to me and I transferred him back to his own chair. They were able to report that Donovan fell and "his friend" had called for help. The actual story had to wait until Donovan was rested and recovered. I later wrote a strongly worded letter to the airport administrators outlining my disgust at the treatment and discrimination I felt Donovan had received. I suggested that the entire airport staff undergo sensitivity training—or at least learn how to recognize a fallen person—perhaps through the use of a series of flash cards or a demonstration with role-play. I heard nothing back and did not expect to, until I did. An airport representative, an underwriter, wanted to discuss what had happened. He came to the house and asked if I could relay what had happened at the airport. Donovan was sitting with us, so I asked Mr. Underwriter if he would like to ask my husband directly since it was his experience. He stammered a bit then redirected the conversation to include Donovan. He wanted to know if the airport was at fault for the fall.

No.

ALS was the culprit, but the lack of accommodation, assistance, or basic human decency by the airport personnel was a contributing factor. The fact that several airport staff walked past a man lying on the ground without inquiring about his well-being was horrendous. Mr. Underwriter nodded in agreement and said that we had valid concerns. He would be in touch, but I was not sure why. Months later, we received a letter from the airport stating that the fall was not their fault and that was the end of the matter.

The falls were numerous, as were the injuries that ranged from scrapes and bruises to broken bones and broken pride. When Donovan lost his balance at home and fell face-first on the kitchen floor, he was unable to put his hands out to save himself. His face broke the fall, and actually broke. The boys had seen their dad fall plenty of times, but that was the first fall where blood burst from Donovan's face, on impact. He lay on the kitchen floor, arms by his sides with a growing pool of blood below him. When he rotated his head to the side, his eyes had squeezed shut under the blood that covered his face. Donovan-Rhys squeezed his blankie to his face and ran to his room. Dylan didn't move from his spot in front of the TV but, without looking in his direction, did ask, "Are you dead, Dad?" His dad replied, "No, Son. Not yet." I pulled Donovan into a sitting position and assessed his injuries. He had an open split across the bridge of his nose from which blood was oozing. His eyes were bloodshot, and blue bruises were forming around them.

"I've seen worse," I lied and pressed a cloth to his face. "Gimme a sec; I'll be back. I have to check on the boy." I went into Donovan-Rhys's room and climbed the first few rungs of his loft bed ladder until I could see him.

"Oh, thank goodness I have found you. I need some help, please. Could you go to the bathroom and bring me a facecloth from under the sink?" I walked out of his room and waited for a moment until I was sure he was coming, then grabbed a towel to clean up as much mess as I could. He sheepishly came into the kitchen where I folded the cloth he brought and swapped it out for the blood-soaked one on his dad's face. "Hold this here; press quite hard. You look after Dad for a minute while I get a plaster." Donovan reassured his son that he was okay, and when I came back, Donovan-Rhys reported on how he had almost stopped the bleeding while his dad filled me in on the best nursing job ever. We high-fived the teamwork and sent him to play with his brother while I closed the wound with Steri-Strips and cleaned the blood. "This could probably use some actual stitches," I said, during my precision injury care.

Donovan replied, "I want to sit in a hospital waiting room about as much as I want a hole in my face."

We all fall down.

For some, at least for me, the uncontrolled descent is not physical. My loss of balance was usually emotionally founded; a poor reaction as opposed to a preconceived action—although I'm sure those who know me would strongly disagree, citing my clumsiness as exceeding that of the average adult. On this occasion, after this fall, I marveled at my husband. He often cried and shared the saddest, most heartfelt sorrow about not being the dad he wanted to be. About not being able to wrestle or throw a ball. Yes, I get it. Physical play is traditionally a dad attribute but could easily be, and was altered to become, a mum thing and a Grampy Wales thing. Surely, long before we were doing it, mums and grampys were making excellent dads, as were many other substitutes. Throwing a ball doesn't make a great dad; letting your seven-year-old boy hold pressure on a wound that probably needed the attention of a medical professional does. Showing your little boy that fear is manageable when we are a team does. Putting your pain—physical, broken nose pain—on hold to manage the pain of your child does. Showing your child that it's okay to ask for help and that it's okay to be helped, saying, " I was scared too. I'm glad we did this together, Son," does. Those are great dad moments. My boys didn't get to have a traditional dad, but for a short while, they had the best dad.

CHAPTER 13

Ashes to Eyelashes

SEVERAL DAYS AFTER THE FUNERAL, the crematorium called to say that Donovan's ashes were ready to be collected.

The ashes weren't ready for the day of the funeral; they had been "created" but not "sifted." I was more than slightly horrified that there was a sifting process. Sifted for what? Does an employee scoop ash into a sieve then tap the side to separate the fine ash from the larger pieces? What are the larger pieces? Donovan didn't have any artificial body parts that I was aware of, but I would imagine that metal head plates or artificial joints would be big enough to just fish right out, no? I mean, you wouldn't want Grandma's ashes sitting in an urn on the mantel with the lid askew due to a metal hip sticking out of the top, would you? What I am trying to say is obviously the big, identifiable bits need to go, but this sifting step was an unpleasant surprise to me.

Unprepared ashes the day of the funeral is apparently quite common. However, I did not know this and was disturbed that the big jar representing Donovan, placed front and center at his funeral surrounded by flowers, was, in fact, empty. I checked. Did everyone know about this charade? People filtered into the church touching the jar of deception on their way by and wept.

Weird.

Ole Sympathy Eyes, the funeral director, tilted his head to the side, touched my arm, managed a smile that showed concern and pity (while excusing my stupidity at not knowing shit about death), and explained that, "This happens all the time." And it wasn't even my jar! It was borrowed from the funeral home, and by *borrowed* I mean rented for a ton of money. This "rental" also contributed to the total cost of the funeral, which was an insane amount of money, considering I had none.

My financial state was never more evident than at my first funeral home visit. The sales staff presented to me their most luxurious, satin-lined coffins, finished in walrus tusk or beaver's teeth and bedazzled with my choice of blood diamonds or Swarovski crystals. I was escorted around the showroom and given information about the unique qualities of each one and why they would make a "perfect tribute to my loved one." They had wildly inflated price tags —thousands of dollars—and the higher the price tag, the better the story about the material used to make it. They had earned their place in ceremonial funeral history. I watched the hopes of that lucrative sale drain from their faces as, much to their horror, I asked if Donovan could be cremated without a coffin. They tried to hide their shock and asked what I would like to use instead. "Would it be possible to use nothing? I think that would be the environmentally responsible choice."

"No, I'm afraid not. He must be contained."

"How about a cardboard box?" They laughed politely, thinking that this was some terrible joke brought on by some atypical widow psychosis. *Ha ha! The joke is on you, death sales lady! I don't have any money for you to take, and you already picked up the body. No "returnsies."*

According to coffin makers and sellers, a cardboard box coffin is illegal and below the minimum standard. Not feeling judged at all, I wondered, *Why on earth would I pay thousands of dollars for something to put in the fire?* We finally agreed on a "combustible container." This was one step and four hundred and fifty dollars (or about ten thousand in today's money) more than the cardboard box—and it met the minimum standard of the burning people law, which I'm sure they made up.

On a rainy, blustery afternoon, the sifted ashes were ready for collection. As with most things, I thought this out in an appropriately sad and romanticized way. I would have my hair swept up, with perfect makeup and wearing a long black coat with matching shoes. I would dash from my car to the cover of the vestibule, ready to collect the small, velvet drawstring pouch filled with ashes. For those who had requested some, I would take a pinch of ash and fold each pinch between layers of fine tissue paper, then tuck the tissue into an embossed envelope with a thoughtful, personalized note before delivery. The rest of the ashes would then be planted below a beautiful miniature pussy willow in our backyard.

Here's what actually happened: I pulled up at the curb, next to a NO PARKING sign. But it's okay—I put my four-ways on. I left the car running, told the kids not to get abducted, and ran into the funeral home, braless, with my unwashed hair in a ponytail. That velvet drawstring pouch was actually a large, plastic-lined cardboard box with six and a half pounds of ashes inside. *Six and a half pounds!* I stood in the reception area of the funeral home and a young lady retrieved the box from a shelf behind her and ripped a Post-it Note from the box with Donovan's name on it.

"Here you go." She smiled and pushed the box my way as if I had been waiting for a much-anticipated delivery.

"Oooh. That's quite heavy."

"That's what most people think." She made and annoyingly pouty face and nodded in agreement with me as she continued to explain. "It's the crushed bone. It's really dense. It makes the ash much heavier than, like, regular campfire ashes."

"That's good to know, thanks."

I thought about refusing the ashes on the grounds of an unacceptable container that didn't meet minimum standards, but the boys might be in the middle of being abducted. Or, more likely, driving off while fighting over who gets to steer. I got back in the car and put the box in the passenger seat. The boys asked what was in the box. I cried and laughed simultaneously because they sounded like Brad Pitt in the movie *Seven*, and also because the answer was, "It's your dad—he is bigger than I expected."

I scooped generic Ziploc baggies full of ashes for those who wanted some and labeled the bags with a Sharpie. The rest would be brought outside for planting. My mother, sister, the boys, and I planned a small, private ceremony and tree planting for Donovan. The boys and I took an emotional trip to the garden center and had already carefully selected the perfect tree. After trying to push each other into a display fountain, sword fighting with branches they ripped from an expensive-looking sapling, and trying to catch koi fish to throw at each other, the boys selected a really lovely Japanese maple. I looked at the three-hundred-and-fifty-dollar price tag (about ten thousand in today's money) and told them that, sadly, we had the wrong type of soil for that breed of tree. Yes, I lied to my children while we were out buying a living monument to their dead father. I ask you to remember that I was poor, and my children were trying to throw live fish at each other. They were then forced to settle on a lovely—but still overpriced—miniature pussy willow so we could leave the damn garden center. I pinched the bridge of my nose while paying to stop myself from shouting profanities at Dylan who was mimicking the fountain statue of a little boy peeing into a pond. Thank the Lord I included them in this monumental tree-purchasing moment. I'm sure they will remember it forever.

I followed the directions for planting, dug the appropriately sized hole for the root ball, and left the little tree next to it. When it was time, we filtered out of the house and into the backyard, already in tears, plastic bag-lined box of ashes in hand. This goodbye was for us. No dressing up, no order of hymns and readings, just our little family creating a place where we could visit and imagine Donovan to be listening. We headed over to the pre-dug hole. I opened up the box containing his ashes and we would take turns scooping some out before releasing them gently into the bottom of the hole in hopes they would nourish our tree and bring a bit of Donovan back to life in each leaf. We each told Donovan that we missed him along with some other words that maybe we forgot to say. We told him that we had selected a spot where he could watch his boys grow and play and be their happiest. When it was Dylan's turn, he didn't gently lower his hand into the ground and release his ashes. He held his arm straight out, at shoulder level in front of him, and released his fist full of ashes both way above the hole and directly into the wind, which blew the ashes straight onto us. For a second, we stood perfectly still and silent, contemplating what we were supposed to do while covered in the ashes of a dead person. We looked at each other, confirming the severe level of ash coverage. We were white. Dylan gasped and covered his mouth with his ashy hand as the rest of us coughed, sputtered, and tried to regain vision. Then we laughed. We patted down our coats and shook

Donovan from our hair and laughed from inside our dust clouds. We knew that, from wherever he was watching, he would be laughing too. I'm not sure how much pull he would have gained with Mother Nature in his short time on the other side, but it's quite possible that he may have had a say in wind speed and direction at the very second Dylan opened his hand. We lost a fist full of Donovan to the wind in the most innocent of actions, turning a somber goodbye into a hilarious farewell.

Dylan made this moment unforgettably perfect; these are the moments we remember and retell. When people said things like, "I don't know how you ever managed," this is how. By laughing at the things that are actually funny even when they happen at the least funny times. By embracing the chaos—because why would death make that change? By giving each other permission to feel deeply, and show it, no matter how that presented itself. By having a family that would share the crazy, the happy, and the sad. It was okay to cry, to be angry and scream, but also, it was really okay to laugh.

The majority of the ashes made it to the intended target and the tree was successfully planted. And, for the rest of the evening, we would find small bits on each other or find ash on an unwiped eyelash and claim that it was "just a bit of Dad."

∽ ∽ ∽

It was late fall when the tree was planted and the leaves soon fell, leaving it bare—which made the tree and me a good match. I hoped for both of us to recover from the shock of being "transplanted," and I had hopes that both the tree and I could manage to grow and come back stronger. The following spring while I was in the yard on "post-snow poo patrol," I noticed furry catkins covering the branches. I ran my hands along the branches and felt the soft, velvety bumps of them slide between my fingers, so happy to feel the abundance of life—and triumphant that we had made it through the harshest of winters.

CHAPTER 14

Happy Anniversary

WE DIDN'T KNOW HOW MANY MILESTONES or occasions we would have. No one does, of course, but I knew that we would have fewer than a regular lifetime full. Every Christmas and every New Year that passed, I wondered if it would be our last. The prognosis for an ALS patient is, on average, three to five years from the time of diagnosis. On the year of our tenth wedding anniversary, we were very much on borrowed time.

All holidays and occasions were celebrated and shared with Donovan's family. Until my mother moved to Canada from Wales to help me take care of Donovan, I had no family with whom to split our holiday time so it made sense that we would celebrate with his family. His dad and stepmother, his two sisters and their families shared the responsibility, along with us, of grand and chaotic Thanksgivings and Christmases with way too much food, probably too much booze, and definitely too many kids running around. It was noisy and busy and wonderful. When my mum did move to Canada, she was simply added to the mix. The tradition was so well established that we knew precisely who would be bringing each dish. Broccoli casserole had to be made by Donovan's older sister; no one could make it like her. Mashed potatoes duty went to his younger sister; they were so good that most people would be happy eating only potatoes for dinner. The only question remaining was who would be hosting, which wasn't difficult to determine either, because we took it in turns. This was how the tradition went for all special occasions and holidays. That is, until the Christmas following Donovan's death. Mum, the boys, and me joined the family for dinner as usual but were told that *this would be the last one we were invited to*, now that Donovan was gone.

Yup, that's right; voted off the island.

Our anniversary was different. It was just ours. No big family celebration; no big celebration at all—but this year was *ten* years. Ten was more years than we thought we'd have so it was a big deal. I wanted a big deal. Donovan was in a wheelchair but still had strength in his legs. He was able to stand with assistance and even walk short distances with help. I could still get him in and out of the car and into or out of his wheelchair on my own. These were manageable restrictions when I began event planning for our anniversary. I had an idea of how I wanted the evening to go. I wanted to re-create the night Donovan asked me to stay in Canada. I was sure that if I planned enough, made some modifications and substitutions, I could find what I needed for this to work. Granted, it would be the grown-up/disabled version of that night, with approximately 100 percent less sex, but that is because one of us was grown-up/disabled and none of us were having sex. But still, we could reconnect, remember the love, and focus on us instead of ALS for just one night.

The first task was to find a babysitter. My group of friends ran home day cares along with me. None of us liked to ask the others to watch our children on their time off; we didn't even want to watch our own children on our days off, but given the situation, my friend stepped up and agreed to have the boys for a sleepover. Yay!! I was secretly scheming and calling various places and my plan was taking shape. By the time the day came, I was prepared for pretty much anything. I told Donovan early in the day that we would be going out. This gave him time to run all of the worst-case scenarios by me, which I was ready for with rehearsed answers—and all of the appropriate equipment was packed in the car to deal with said scenarios. The day prior, I had packed medical supplies and pills while he was napping so he would have no idea what I was up to. I made sure that there was plenty of time to get us both ready. I helped Donovan into a pair of regular jeans with a button and a zip closure. He wore an external catheter with the drainage bag secured on his lower leg so there would be no need to worry about the bathroom. When he was ready to go, I went into the bathroom, put on makeup, and did my hair. I put on clothes that required ironing and a pair of shoes that I would have to take off to drive. I stared at myself in the mirror and said "there you are" to the hottie I hardly recognized staring back at me. I was straightening the straps on my borrowed, sexy black shirt as I walked into the kitchen, about to corral the boys to the car, when I intercepted a trans-kitchen shootout. Had I been one second later, I would have missed the straw full of milk that Dylan spewed at his brother. Instead, the Gods of Ill-Fated Timing guided me to a direct hit to the chest. I looked like a throwback to breastfeeding days. "Get in the car," I growled through gritted teeth as the boys ran and I went to my closet and selected the least pilled or stained top that I could find.

Putting the wardrobe sabotage behind us, we dropped the boys off and started our evening. We began by going out for dinner. I called ahead to a gorgeous little restaurant that came recommended and I explained our situation. The owner had kindly prepared a table in a private area for us where I could discreetly feed Donovan without prying eyes. Understandably, Donovan didn't want to be fed in public so we didn't eat out—ever. And because he needed feeding, we didn't eat together. I fed him dinner then usually shoveled food into my mouth while cleaning the kitchen. This dinner out was a luxurious treat that I had been saving for by skimming from my day care pay for months. Meals were cooked to perfection; Donovan even sipped a glass of red wine from a straw. We took our time and had an actual conversation. For the first time in a very long time, we talked about memories instead of tasks; we were relaxed and uninterrupted. We smiled at each other and remembered that we had married for love—the memory took a little dusting off, but it was there. We enjoyed each moment of our meal and shared a crème brûlée before asking for the check. When it arrived, our server silently placed it face down on the table, then wrapped her arms around my husband from behind, then did the same to me before scurrying out of sight. I gave a confused smile/shrug to Donovan as I reached for the bill; it read ZERO as the amount owing. Like our server, the owner came to our table and hugged us both. They said that they were the ones who were thankful. They thanked us for letting them be a part of this occasion, and picking up the tab was their pleasure. I wanted to express my gratitude but was crying so mostly squeaks and whines came out when I tried. They probably regretted it somewhat when, as I was wheeling Donovan through the main dining area, through other diners, to leave the restaurant, I made the rookie mistake of trying to wipe my drippy nose while pushing the wheelchair. I one-handed swerved his chair, and him, into a man who was drinking from a pint glass. There was some minor spillage and an awkward moment of untangling the two, but we eventually made it outside.

"Apart from that last bit, that was perfect. Thank you," Donovan said as I wrestled him into the car.

"Let me see if I can make up for that last bit." I was so proud of myself for A) keeping a secret this long and B) for having another surprise on deck. "It's not over yet."

I folded up the wheelchair and stowed it. I hopped into the front seat with a smug grin and, without being asked, turned, grabbed his cheeks, and yelled, "You'll have to wait and see! Stop pressuring me!" It was just a short drive before we pulled up at our destination.

"Ta-daaaaa!"

I had brought us back to the motel where Donovan had first asked me to stay with him. The forecourt had been paved and the motel had been painted a pastel color. Other than that, it was the same; there were bulbs burned out on the sign and I could hear the rough waters of Lake Ontario crashing against the rocks at the back of the motel. I had brought the same music and the same beer, but with straws. I could hardly contain my excitement.

"Let me go and check us in." I kissed his cheek and headed to the lobby before he could start the barrage of questions about how we would manage.

I returned to the car a few minutes later, crying for the second time that evening, this time a bad cry. Our room had been given to someone else; our new room was now on the second floor, accessible only by the exterior metal staircase. I explained, pleaded, and produced proof of my monthlong reservation before becoming a little upset. The man at reception thought my demands of removing the people from our original room were an overreaction; I thought he should eat shit and die, and this brought our conversation to a close.

Instead of lighting the shitty motel on fire, I drove home. I was sad and frustrated but Donovan was relieved; he appreciated the thought but needed the comfort and routine of home. When I unpacked the car, he realized that I had brought just about everything he would have needed to be comfortable. His head pillow, his leg pillows, sheepskin pads, medications, external catheter supplies, oral care, powders, creams, and so on.

"Wow," he said. "You brought so much stuff from home, we might as well be here." I think he was trying to make it okay that we were back at home but I felt like I had wasted a great deal of time and effort on a stupid idea.

"I'm not a wife at home. I thought a change of scenery might remind us that we are more than a patient and a carer." I sobbed and dramatically smeared makeup across my face with a cloth.

"I know we forget it in the day-to-day stuff," Donovan offered. "I should tell you more often that you are so much more to me than a carer. Let me see if I can help. Go in my power chair bag—there is something in there for you." I hustled my mascara-smudged face over to his power chair and retrieved a small box from the bag that hung on the back. It was from a jewelry shop in town.

When Donovan's disability check arrived, he had the postman put it in his wheelchair bag; the other mail went in the box. He would then drive his chair into town and take his check to the bank, usually with one of the boys sitting on his lap or hanging on to the back of his chair. The boys or a teller would go into the bag for him and get the check deposited. For months, while doing this, he took some of the checks as cash, had the teller put it in an envelope in his bag, then drove his chair from the bank to the jewelers.

There, he had the store owner go into his bag and retrieve the money to put toward a piece of jewelry he had on layaway. He visited the jewelers every check day until the debt was paid. It felt like a collaborative town crusade led by my husband. He had never put such an effort into a surprise and picked a time in his life when he was least able to do it. Yet, his quest was unstoppable, and on our tenth anniversary, Donovan gave me a gold ring with ten diamonds channel set into the band. One for each year of our marriage. I never had an engagement ring; I had never had a nice piece of jewelry until this most perfect gift. The day had been a roller coaster of events and emotions, much like our lives.

"I'm sorry tonight didn't go as planned," he said. "But I'm not sure that we can re-create things. We can't go back in time and have what we used to; we can only make the most of what we have now."

"I miss us," I told him. "I know nothing can be done about it; I just do. This ring is beautiful and perfect. I love you. I know how much effort you put into getting it."

I slid my anniversary ring onto my finger and pretended not to feel a slap of nasty reality. I thought I was re-creating a perfectly romantic evening when what I was actually doing was forcing my disabled husband into being uncomfortable in unfamiliar surroundings because I longed for something that was gone. I let my imagination wander and thought that somehow we would get a onetime ALS hall pass. Although we had not lost love, we had laid to rest an intimacy—the spark of which I thought even the darkest of circumstances could never extinguish. The idea was an impossible fantasy that was doomed to fail. The booking error at the motel saved me from actually facing the fact that had we made it into the magical room, where there would be no dancing or lovemaking—there would simply be the typical nighttime routine except more uncomfortable and less accessible. I had been foolish and failing in the practicality I practiced and lived by, every single day. I was embarrassed that I so enthusiastically tried to force a round peg into a hole that had become square.

I thought love could outweigh disability.

Except, when one is an amateur boxer and one is an army tank, it's not a fair fight. Embarrassed that I wanted to sleep in a bed next to my husband when illness had deemed it impossible. Embarrassed that I thought I could turn back time. The day marked the tenth anniversary of our wedding. It was against all odds that we'd made it this far; medical professionals said so. Should I have been silently happy that we hadn't lost more? Should I have shut down my damn whining about intimacy, or sex, or of a caring touch? Should I have thanked my lucky stars that we even had this milestone to celebrate?

Fuck you, lucky stars. And fuck you, ALS.

CHAPTER 15

Taxes

CANADIAN TAXES ARE COMPLEX AND tedious. I hate tax time with a passion—with the possible exception of my very first attempt when I got drunk and calculated that the government owed me almost $8,000 (they didn't). It is, inarguably, a hideous task. I plan on waffling on about it for some time in this chapter. If you're my family, especially my parents, children, or husband, you have probably heard this all before.

Go ahead, skip this chapter. I forgive you.

If you're still reading, then the actual truth is that I am going to be talking about sex. *My sex life*, to be exact. If you're my family, especially my parents, children, or husband, this is your second chance to opt out. Please take it.

You have been fully forewarned.

When is the right time to start dating, start a relationship—or just have sex—post spousal death? When does the ring come off? Everyone has an opinion. Those opinions range from, "You're young. Get back in the saddle" (I'm going to assume that the saddle here is dating), to, "That was your one true love; there can be no other." Or, "One year. That's the standard—everyone knows."

I didn't know... but what I did know was that the loneliness was crushing. Not just the loneliness that death brings but also the loneliness that terminal illness had created.

Donovan had ALS for nine years. It didn't just rob him of his life; it robbed him of so much more. He couldn't be a hockey dad or throw a ball. He couldn't wrestle with his boys, and when they read a book together, the boys turned the pages. He also couldn't touch his wife. Not a bum pinch while passing in the kitchen, not an embrace for when you're happy or sad, and certainly not sex.

There wasn't a calendar day with an X through it to mark *THE END OF SEX* day. Like many things ALS stole, it was subtle at first—manageable with some patience and a position change or two. After a while, though, the effort exceeded the pleasure. And since we were both so very tired—him from living with a terminal illness, and me from taking care of someone with a terminal illness—sex took an unquestionably clear back seat. Once it became physically impossible, sex became a one-sided service from which I was detached, and then resentful. There were some conversations around the fairness of the situation and wifely duty and it was at a time when control was being frantically clung to for dear life. Demands for certain sexual services came with threats of turning to someone who would be paid for a positive outcome should I fail to satisfy the most basic of human needs. His hands had long since betrayed him; therefore, he was unable to provide himself with any gratification. And so the desperate demands were made. Ultimately the objections were surrendered as ALS won another battle. You see, my husband didn't die all at once; ALS caused multiple small deaths throughout the years before rendering the final blow.

When my husband died, I hadn't experienced intimacy in about five years. No one had touched my face and kissed me; I had not felt skin against mine. It had occurred to me that I might never meet someone and I might never have sex again. The thought of that was terrifying but so was the prospect of actually learning to date again. Since I somehow missed receiving my copy of *This Is What to Do When You're a New Widow,* and social media was but a twinkle in Zuckerberg's eye, I put those thoughts on the back burner and took my boys to Blockbuster Video.

However, after some time and lots of persuasion, I did try going on a couple of dates. Bad Date Number One: A blind date set up by a friend to meet someone in a local pub, making it easy to just have a drink and part ways—or stay and order food if things went well. I loved that idea and had a well-rehearsed exit strategy. I arrived five minutes early hoping to be seated before he arrived, but dammit all; he was there, sitting in a booth. Our eyes met as I was explaining to the hostess that I was meeting someone, and I swear, time slowed down. He stood from the table, smiled, and waved me over. He was basically Luke Perry when he was in *90210*—like, really, really hot. So far out of my league that I relaxed and assumed that we would both immediately arrive at the same conclusion. He was sweet enough not to spit his drink back into his glass and flee upon meeting me. Instead, he was kind, funny, and very good company. We chatted, keeping it on the lighter side, and shared some laughs. Then, to my complete surprise, he flagged down a server and asked for a menu.

What the . . . ? Was this turning into a dinner date?

TGFMG (too gorgeous for me guy): "You are funny and smart and gorgeous. Wanna have some dinner?"

Me: "I think that would be nice."

Way to play it cool. High five, me!

We continued to talk and I sat in amazement at how well this was going, and how easy it was to connect with another man. I was having a good time. Maybe a little too good. It felt a little wrong, a little like cheating.

Oh, shut up, brain; enough with the cock blocking!

I scolded myself back to the conversation as the food arrived. His meal arrived first; the server placed it and said she would be right back with mine. He immediately began eating. My food did come right out by which time it was clearly established that this man had the table manners of a scavenging turkey vulture. For every bite he shoveled into his mouth, he pulled the food from his fork by scraping it through his teeth. With every bite, I shuddered. I smiled and was polite instead of screaming "Chew with your damn mouth shut!" while stabbing him in the chin with my fork.

We did not date again.

Bad Date Number Two: (SKGGD guy—sweet, kind, generous, good daddy). I feel bad for labeling this one as a bad date. It was 100 percent my picky issues that made it so. Nonetheless, I feel that his failure to pay proper attention to wardrobe details caused our ultimate demise. It was a man that I had semi-known; our children had, on occasion, been on the same sports team. He approached me one day and introduced himself, then followed the introduction with, "If I wanted to get to know you better, would I ask you out on a date? Would I get someone to ask for me? Should I send a note home with your son? I'm not sure how this works."

"Oooh, dating advice. You have come to the right place."

"Really?"

"No. I am the last person you should ask, but since you did, I would say you should probably just ask."

"Okay, cool, thanks." He then walked off—and went back to his folding chair. He came back at the end of the game and said, "Hi. I'm Ian. Would you like to come on a date with me?" Funny fucker, this one.

"No thank you."

"Oh, right."

"I'm just messing with you. I would like that."

He picked me up and took me to a pretty waterfront town where a festival was taking place. We walked through the crowded vendors and stopped to look at the work of local artists. We shared snacks from different food trucks and discovered our mutual love of extra-judgy people watching. We stopped to play games and Ian gave me his prize teddy. It was during this prize-winning moment that the seemingly perfect date unraveled. Ian, who was sweet, kind, generous, a great daddy—and, to top it off, ate with his mouth closed—was reaching to throw a wooden ball at some stacked cans. That is when I saw it. Flashing between his black shoes and trousers were white tube gym socks. A little wave of disappointment washed over me as Ian proudly passed me the teddy.

We did not date again.

The following spring after Donovan's death, the boys and I went to Nanaimo, British Columbia, to visit their half-sister, Kylee. We stayed with her mum, who was Donovan's ex-wife. I know, right? I'm a weirdo! Well, you judgmental bunch, let me tell you a little about ex-wife Charlotte. What happened in their marriage is none of my business (it took me a while to learn that), except they did have a beautiful daughter, Kylee. This beautiful daughter had a long-distance relationship with her daddy, who she loved very, very much. So much effort was made by everyone to foster that relationship with summer visits and letter writing. When Donovan's illness had progressed to the point where death seemed like it was serious about making an appearance, I had a conversation with Charlotte. We talked about Kylee and if she needed to come and see her dad. We talked about Donovan needing to see his daughter. If she did come, would she come alone? Kylee was sixteen years old and this might be the last time she would see her dad. How on earth do I put this little girl on a plane, alone, after saying goodbye to her dad, probably for the last time?

The solution was simple: Charlotte would be coming

too; there is no way she could let her daughter go through any of this without her mum by her side. Of course not. I was relieved for Kylee but also a bit scared for me. For Charlotte and me, this would be our first time meeting. Not that it should be the substance of worry. I most definitely had other things going on. But despite appearing to be a genderless caregiver robot, I did have regular, every-woman insecurities, damn it. I was, at best, a frazzled mess and she was something out of a magazine. Let me put it this way—her hair was beautiful, her makeup was perfect, and her nails were done. I had never, in my life, had a manicure. I don't know how to make the picture any clearer than that.

Kylee and Charlotte were extended celebrity status and closely guarded while being hosted by the in-laws. When she arrived at my house with the in-law entourage, she had the biggest, most beautiful smile. It made me realize why I'd been told I don't smile enough. I had a palm-to-forehead ah-ha moment. Comparison. Younger me would have taken it harder. The version of me that put the pieces together when Charlotte and I first met shrugged her shoulders and thought, *Well, you're stuck with me now.* There was, of course, a teary reuniting and the inevitable shock of seeing Donovan's deterioration, but when the dust settled, Charlotte looked around and asked, without a moment's hesitation, where she could be of use. Noticing the overgrown lawn, she quietly acknowledged that we weren't getting enough help.

"There are teenage boys in this family—why on earth would the grass get so long?" She generically threw that out there on her way to the shed. Before anyone could say "rude bitch," or before I could say "wait, let me make you tea," she had fired up the mower and was damn well making herself useful.

That is a very fleeting introduction to Charlotte, but I could see why Donovan had loved her. I could see why she was too much of a badass boss to fit in with his family. I thought she was pretty fab and I knew that, whatever happened, Kylee would grow up to be brave and strong and oh so loved.

We were welcomed and treated like royalty in BC. Charlotte and I spent hours talking; it was good therapy. We lounged in her hot tub and I poured my heart out to her while her husband brought us cocktails. This was her actual life, people! She worked hard, was madly in love with her amazing husband, and kept tabs on two beautifully happy girls. At the end of her busy day, she did things like going for a nice walk or playing a round of golf—or relaxing in that sweet hot tub.

Strange.

I thought everyone ran around like a maniac cleaning and preparing for the next day once the kids and husband were in bed. At no point did I see her microwaving and scarfing a frozen pasta dinner at 10:00 p.m.

I could get used to the hot tub life. This is where she told me about a "really great guy" and wanted me to meet him. No pressure, just see how it feels to chat with someone. *Sure, no big deal. I can talk to a man.*

Also, how do I go about changing my flight so I can go home and become a celibate hermit?

At a casual backyard BBQ, the mystery man—having been fed the backstory—came over, leaned himself on the picnic table next to me, and offered one of the two drinks he was holding. He was charming, had a Jon Bon Jovi smile, and was, well, a bit of all right. I, on the other hand, suddenly discovered that English was, in fact, my second language. I somehow managed not to scare him away and we arranged to do this again the following night.

Just a casual get-together with friends.

That evening, I began to realize how other adults and families lived in the absence of an all-consuming illness. My boys ran around, carefree and laughing, and I had uninterrupted adult conversations. No outstanding tasks were setting tiny fires in my brain. It felt foreign, but good. Was I relaxed? Was this actual relaxation? I couldn't be sure; part of me wanted to sample this other life and part of me wanted to crumble under the weight of the guilt I felt when I absent-mindedly reached for the wedding band I had taken off before leaving for this trip.

My boys bounced over to announce a newly hatched bedtime plan involving a scary movie, a bunch of kids, and probably very little sleep. I was excusing myself to be the teeth-brushing monitor and remind them not to break anything when Charlotte shot me the "Don't you dare" stare, and waved me off.

"I've got this," she shouted over her shoulder. The boys followed, running inside and not even looking back. So, wow! Now I'm kind of on a date and I have no excuse not to be fully present. JBJSG (Jon Bon Jovi Smile Guy, whose name was actually Raj) and I talked and laughed and held each other's gaze a little too long. I marveled at his Snuffleupagus-ish eyelashes. He brushed the back of my hand with his thumb and I didn't pull away. He moved close to ask if I wanted a drink and moved my hair over my shoulder, and, as he did so, let his hand rest on my back. I enjoyed the touch, and the light, warm pressure of his hand that covered a big area of my back. I felt the warmth radiate through my body. My tiny neck hairs tingled and I wondered if he could feel the goose bumps through my thin shirt. These gentle test touches continued and I was torn between what my body craved and what my confused brain was telling me. I wanted to move into this touch; I wanted to feel more of him and surrender to this hunger. I wanted to run away and hide behind the safety of my cold, arm's-length fear. On my way back from the bathroom, he caught me, alone.

I was trapped.

Stuck between the washer and dryer, bathroom door and him. He stood close, like right in my personal space, and said, "I should probably kiss you." I'm pretty sure he was using the Jon Bon Jovi smile as a weapon. It worked. I replied, "I agree, you probably should." My stomach was in knots and I could hear my heart pounding. I said a silent prayer to the First Date Gods: *Please, oh please, don't let me throw up in his face.* He leaned in but instead of kissing me, he lifted me up and sat me on the dryer. I was then slightly worried about a back injury as well as the possibility of facial vomit, but before I could muster a sarcastic comment to alleviate my awkwardness, he pushed my thighs apart, pressed himself against me.

He took my face in his hands and kissed me.

On the drive to his house, Raj pointed out that I was quiet. Since there was a decent chance that this guy was about to see me naked, I figured I should at least manage his expectations. I told him that I was a little scared. I told him that it had been a very long time and that I was basically a virgin and probably didn't remember how to "do" sex at all. He did the Jon Bon Jovi smile, brought my hand to his mouth, and kissed it. He said all of the right things. He said we could drink tea and watch trash TV if that's what I wanted. We could break out the instruments and play band hero if that's what I wanted.

So, we had sex.

He led me to his bedroom. We undressed each other, kissed our way onto his bed, and had sex. And the greatest thing—it wasn't awkward (yet). There were things I loved about being with him, the heat and weight of his body on mine, the feel of his hands on my skin. Just being caressed was so unfamiliar, yet its memory came crashing back to me in a huge, emotional sex wave. He was thoughtful and generous, but the actual sex was . . . meh. I wasn't sure if it was my mind or my vagina that was broken. Probably both. I kept thinking that at any second my vagina would spring into action, and I would feel some arousal, a twitch, anything . . .

Hello?? Is this thing on?

The fact that this conversation was going on inside my head, during sex, while I was simultaneously wondering when it would be over, was concerning. The saying "use it or lose it" apparently applies to vaginas, as mine was lost. That beautiful Bon Jovi smile melted into a loud, mouth-breathing sleep. His heavy arm was draped across my chest, seriously squishing my left boob, and my arm was trapped under his neck. As panic set in, I briefly looked around for something sharp to sever my arm because that would have been preferable to waking him. Since there was nothing, I decided to do the next best, rational thing. I fake stretched and rolled. When there was no movement, I continued the roll, all the way out of bed. He was sleeping like a . . . guy who just got laid.

This stealthy bitch gathered up a ball of clothes and tip-toed to the door. I reached for the handle and froze. Jesus! Why, in a new, suburban house, did the bloody door hinges screech like they were from 1828? I held my breath and checked—still nothing. I slid through the smallest opening I could manage, rotating myself to check back on the slack-faced mouth breather one last time, and then exited onto the landing.

Nailed it!

I turned to head to the bathroom, ball of clothes in hand, *only to come face-to-face with a naked teenaged boy*. Oh my good God!

I gasped. He gasped, open-mouthed, staring at my . . . everything. Then, from behind me I heard, "Oh, hey, Son."

And there was me thinking that enough naked people were standing there, but no, there should definitely be one more entirely naked person to complete the trifecta.

I was so very busted.

Despite that, Raj had brought the bedsheet out with him and draped it around me from behind, then walked me back to a sofa in the bedroom. He closed the door on his son who honestly didn't know if I even had a face. Raj acknowledged that a heads-up about his son being home would have been handy (Oh, you think, Raj?). I acknowledged trying to escape undetected and then wishing for the ground to open up and swallow me. He asked if, in the unlikely event my escape had been successful, did I know where I was going or how I planned to get there? I did not. All I knew at that moment was panic. I thought I was ready for this. Raj offered to drive me back to Charlotte's house right away, if I wanted. Or he would sleep on the couch.

I felt shitty for trying to sneak out. I was suddenly so tired and remembered how good, and how soothing, it was to lie in bed and feel the skin of someone against my own. I asked for that. I asked him to come back to bed. He took my hand, did the Jon Bon Jovi smile, and led the way. *Wait! Oh my God. Was that a twinge? Vajay, is that you?*

In the morning, on the drive home, Raj pointed out that just because my second first time wasn't perfect didn't mean that it wasn't memorable.

CHAPTER 16

The Poisoning

EXPERTS HAVE DETERMINED THAT THE BRAIN remains unaffected by amyotrophic lateral sclerosis. My lie detector has determined that this is a lie. I don't actually have one of those, but I strongly disagree. ALS is the worst disease known to man. I know that you're racking your brain to challenge me on this. There's leprosy, Ebola, necrotizing fasciitis, you'll say. While they are strong contenders, ALS leaves them looking like a nasty cold. ALS destroys the neurons that communicate with muscles, slowly causing them to waste away. This leads to paralysis. The affected slowly lose the ability to walk, move, eat, and eventually breathe. This process usually takes three to five years. For Donovan, it was nine years of suffering.

Nine.

The disease doesn't cause physical destruction of the brain as it does to the rest of the body. However, slowly deteriorating, knowing that death is imminent for a period of three to five—or nine—years can certainly take a toll on mental health.

Healthy Donovan used to be a champion boxer. He fought, and he won. ALS was a contender far out of anyone's league. It bit, eye-gouged, and hit below the belt. It continued throwing dirty, invisible punches long after the bell was rung. My strong, athletic, happy husband became frail, weak, anxious, and depressed. At times his behavior was uncharacteristic and alarming. At times, so was mine.

This became very apparent one Christmas. I was trying to get to a pop-up discount toy store located in Toronto, a forty-five-minute drive away, to shop for the boys. Choreographing such an outing required arranging childcare, as well as care for Donovan. There was a very small pool of people that could manage the physical care he required, and a smaller pool of those he trusted to do so. On my first two attempts to get there, he panicked and had his caregiver call me to come home. On the third attempt, my mum stepped in and assured me that she would not be calling me home. Mum and I went through the plan with Donovan, covered the "what-ifs," and talked through his fears. I told him that I needed this; I needed a morning away. He agreed. I know he wanted this for me, but the power of panic and anxiety could ultimately rule the moment.

My girlfriend April arrived early to pick me up. There was one last request: Donovan asked me to make him a cup of tea and bring him out to the deck. Mum was more than capable of doing this, of course, and we all knew that this was a small grasp at control. He could have it; it was the least I could do to have a morning away and try to tackle some Christmas shopping to-dos. I helped position Donovan's wheelchair at our plastic patio table and pulled the fleece Toronto Maple Leafs blanket over his lap, tucking in his hands. I asked which straw he wanted; he liked different straws for different drinks. I walked onto the deck with my bag on my shoulder, set his cup of tea before him, making sure that he could reach it, then kissed him goodbye. April and I left; we contemplated grabbing coffee but thought the drive-through delay would be tempting fate. She drove as if the distance between home and the toy store was the deciding factor in reaching our destination. The closer we got, the more likely we would make it there uninterrupted. That was not to be. We were at the halfway mark when my old-school mobile phone rang. I pressed the ANSWER button and hoisted that house brick up to my ear. April's head fell back in defeat as I answered the call with, "Are you serious right now?"

"I'm sorry, love." This was the last thing Mum wanted to do. "It got really bad. He demanded an ambulance and he's on his way to the hospital."

"Oh shit. Is he hurt?"

"Not physically, but he is definitely not himself."

Donovan had panicked. He called Mum out to the deck and told her that he didn't feel well. He told her to call me. She offered to bring him in and get him comfortable in his power recliner; he would feel better there.

"No need to call Hayley. Remember the plan," she told him. He declined, stating that he was dying, that there was something wrong with his tea. He was pale, crying, and trying to sway his body as if wanting to fall out of his chair. He struggled to coordinate breathing with the amount of secretions his crying created. As the panic escalated, he repeatedly demanded that Mum call me and an ambulance, in succession. Donovan-Rhys and Dylan watched the unraveling through the window until Mum gave them the very important job of waiting for the paramedics and showing them to the back deck.

April and I turned around and I apologized to her through my tears of frustration. She squeezed my hand, an assurance that we would figure this out. I appreciated her ability to maintain composure instead of screaming, "This is bullshit!" She dropped me in the circular driveway of the hospital's main entrance as the ambulance was pulling in. It backed into its designated spot as I walked over in time for the rear doors to swing open.

As loud as his frailty would allow, Donovan was screaming that I tried to kill him so I could go shopping. His eyes locked on me, and he shouted, "You poisoned my tea! You tried to kill me!"

Something inside of me snapped. Fury and some inexplicable form of madness took over as I publicly cried, "If I had tried to kill you by poisoning your tea, you'd be fucking dead! That's it! I have had a fucking guts full of you! You can fuck off and live with your father. He can deal with you being a psycho!"

Except I still followed him into the ER.

The attending paramedic assured me that he did not believe the poisoning story and he had no concerns about Donovan's care at home. I wondered if he would reconsider this, given my recent claims that I could have fatally poisoned my husband if I had wanted to; not to mention the threats of throwing my terminally ill husband out of our house. Not my finest hour. I asked if he was going to call the police about this alleged, attempted murder. He thought it wouldn't be necessary.

I thought, *Shame. Jail would be a nice break.*

The paramedics remained unphased by Donovan's behavior, but the triage nurse stepped right in with, "Sir! Sir! You *need* to calm down." I have always found that the absolute best way to calm someone down is to tell him or her to calm down—but in this case, strangely, it had the opposite effect. Donovan was wheeled into a room and clumsily transferred to an ER bed while loudly protesting everything that was happening and maintaining that he had been poisoned. I answered some hurried questions about allergies and medical history so the attending physician could sedate him. Nurse Calm Down barked at a security guard to "get the restraints," and I suggested that that might not be necessary. She countered with, "I'll be the judge of that. Safety is the priority here."

"Super. Your diligence is admirable. Donovan has ALS and is absolutely no physical threat." She didn't answer me but did tell security that she wouldn't need the restraints because the situation seemed to have resolved.

I watched as Donovan's anger subsided and gave way to a soft cry as the sedation forced him into submission. He was asleep when an oxygen mask was slipped over his face. It was at that point that I could no longer hold back my tears. They were cried for the anger I felt about the accusation, the sadness I felt for not recognizing the man in front of me, the shame I felt for my outburst, and for everything that was out of my control.

At the same time, a familiar and expected punch in the stomach brought me back to earth. I headed to the bathroom. As I walked, the cramps felt like my uterus was full of ninjas throwing stars at an army of angry crustaceans, snapping their pincers inside me. This was accompanied by a wave of dizziness.

I made it inside the washroom and was cleverly able to lock the door before losing consciousness *on the floor of a public bathroom.*

Someone walking by heard the commotion and alerted a staff member, who alerted a custodian who could override the lock. They also called for assistance from a nurse and a student doctor. When the door opened, all of them were standing there, including the original passerby who was far too invested not to be there for the reveal. I was, fortunately, still unconscious so I didn't have to be aware of what I can only imagine was absolute horror at the sight of me. I had been incontinent, and my period had inconsiderately not held off for this particular crisis to pass. So, there I was, unconscious, lying in a pool of blood and urine *on the floor of a public hospital bathroom.* I had mere seconds of grasping the situation before embarrassment gobbled me up. I asked if everyone could please leave so I could try to contain the mess and possibly preserve a shred of dignity. The answer was a resounding "no." This was further emphasized as I was lifted and placed on a stretcher. What followed was a series of explanations: *I haven't eaten; it's been a stressful morning. I just got my period and I needed to urinate before leaving the house this morning. I really had to go . . .*

Despite all of these perfectly legitimate, compounding reasons for passing out, the student doctor drew his own conclusions. The first and most obvious choice was a shark attack. This was ruled out when tests revealed that we were not in the ocean. The next, less desirable diagnosis was that I had suffered a seizure. I argued that, not only had I *not* had a seizure, but also I wasn't even a patient. My husband was. I was only there because of the alleged poisoning.

Junior doctor wrote SEIZURE on my chart and contacted the Ministry of Transportation (MTO) to report the condition. This action, on this day, marked the beginning of a void of darkness that reached into me with a palpable malevolence. It stirred in me and through me in a way that became so violent, my desperation and sadness spilled out onto people I love, marking them forever.

The Ministry of Transportation immediately took away my driver's license. A later CT scan showed no seizure activity; it indicated nothing but a healthy-looking brain. That may have been a stretch but I definitely did not have a seizure. Please note: I was the only driver in our house. Donovan hadn't been able to drive for a very long time. Mum didn't drive. Correcting the situation and reinstating my license would take time. Until then, I would ask for rides, help with groceries and appointments. I would push a wheelchair through snow and over unplowed curbs. Everything became so much harder during that Canadian winter.

Donovan was alone and groggy when the sedation wore off. His nurse talked to my nurse and visitation was arranged by wheeling me from my bed to his. Once I partially explained what had happened, his confusion gave way to tears. He was sorry and didn't really think that I had tried to kill him. I told him the good news: I wasn't going to be arrested. The bad news: I had lost my license and we were all going to jail. House arrest, to be precise.

My mum, who had been at home with the boys, was stuck. Stuck worrying, wondering what was going on and if she now had me to take care of on top of everything else. She had been contacted by hospital staff about my situation, but the person calling had been unaware of the connection between Donovan and me. For a while, she had to take on so much. All of it, in fact.

In the ER I was (unnecessarily) treated with an anti-seizure medication that left me, let's say, altered and unreliable until it had made its way out. Mum suddenly became responsible for four needy people, and she just did the things that needed to be done. (Thanks, Mum.) It was hard. It was hard before all of this happened, but now we couldn't even fake how difficult our lives had become.

My family doctor, another of life's greatest humans, noticed that I might be struggling when I sobbed in her office and told her that I couldn't carry on. She referred us to community services. Donovan had been against outside help. His needs were private and he did not want some stranger washing his privates. To be honest, I was not too enamored with the idea either. I wasn't overly bothered about someone washing his willy; it was more that I wanted to be strong enough to do it alone. I wanted to do *everything*. I wanted that medal that gets handed out to people that could endure the least sleep and do the most things. Wait. That's not right.

There was no medal.

There was passing out *on the floor of a hospital public restroom* (I will eternally want to shower after saying that) because my body and possibly my brain were sick of trying to give me subtle messages that I ignored. It felt like defeat to have a support worker, but the agency sent one in anyway.

Christine came for three hours every weekday morning; it was someone else on the weekends.

I am embarrassed to say that she came into a hostile environment. We were, all of us, a little resistant to the perceived intrusion. Christine was about my mum's age, had a strong Cockney accent, and a potty mouth. She had a no-nonsense approach and a job to do. I'm not sure how long she was made to feel uncomfortable in my home, but I am sorry for every second.

The poisoning event had led to an unraveling of sorts. It was recognition of limitations and the beginning of some self-care along with accepting outside help. Except Christine didn't stay as outside help. I don't remember when she became a part of our family; there was no particular moment where it was suddenly clear that she was essential. We simply couldn't imagine life without her.

Christine and her husband, Dave, a Cockney champion boxing coach, truly became family to us. Christine and Mum became best friends, and I referred to her as my "Other Mother." Donovan trusted Christine with the most intimate of care and she could manage him on his bad days as well as his good ones. He looked up to Dave who made him part of a boxing family once again, taking him to watch sparring and training. Years earlier, Mum had been the gift to keep me going. She left her home, career, and younger daughter to help me take care of Donovan and our boys—all while reestablishing herself and her career in a new country. Christine brought the same gift, exactly when it was needed most. In her, I found true understanding and empathy.

As the disease took more and more of Donovan, his behavior became unpredictable. He would be cruel at times, demanding that I dial his sister's phone number and then hold the phone up to his mouth while he told her that I was starving him or refusing to care for him. Yes, I would just do it—there was no point in arguing. He would, in his desperate moments of frustration, tell his family that he was forced to wait, be last in line for things, or was being treated poorly. There were times when this carried a shred of truth. I had two small boys and ran a day care from home, but Donovan was *never* last.

I was.

There was one incident that was particularly painful for both of us. It left an indelible mark and the fallout from it changed relationships forever.

I stood Donovan in a well-practiced position and pulled down his elastic-waist fleece pants. We did the pivot/dance that backed his legs against the toilet bowl and I placed him down on the seat. I left to give him a moment alone. When he called me back in, I lifted him to standing and we began the dance in reverse with the added step of leaning his body against the wall to facilitate a cleanup. This cleanup was a little more challenging for me—a little worse. There is no way to delicately describe why it was worse. It was smelly. I was very used to the cleanup; I routinely cleaned a grown man. If you've ever accidentally gone into the bathroom after your husband/dad/brother when they have just had a morning sit-down, you feel me here, and I was hands-on with that shit. I would also routinely walk around picking up the toddlers, one at a time, pressing their bum to my nose to find who needed a change. I was not afraid of poo. I was stoic and controlled, but now and again, there was a bad one.

This was a bad one.

I stood behind Donovan and worked hard on suppressing the gag, keeping it silent so he wouldn't know, but the reaction was physical. He knew. He was so offended, so hurt and embarrassed. I hated myself for making him feel that way, and yet, I couldn't stop. He was angry, and asked if I knew how I was making him feel, and if I knew what kind of person I was. He demanded that I stop, and yet, I couldn't.

"Donovan, I am so"—*gag*—"sorry. I really can't"—*gag*—"help it."

"It really sounds like you're sorry." He was crying. He felt like shit. I felt like shit, all because of shit.

"You're all clean. Let's get you sitting."

"What is wrong with you? Do you know how much I hate that I need you to do this for me? Don't you know I would love to be able to do this myself?"

"I do know. I really do. I couldn't help it."

"Get me the phone." Donovan had me dial his sister's number and he cried to her on the phone. I'm sure she couldn't make out anything he was saying. This was, for her, heartbreaking. When he could speak, he didn't share the embarrassment of the bathroom event; he told her that he could no longer live with cruel mistreatment and added some insults describing neglect. I stood behind his wheelchair so he could lean his head against me—his neck got easily fatigued—and I held the phone up so he could speak.

The thing is, most of the time, Donovan was kind, reasonable, and very grateful when absolutely no thanks were needed. He always apologized for the things he said when he was upset. When he did get upset, it was the maximum possible amount of upset. It was the most abrupt, extreme, and cruelest reaction imaginable.

I am not sure why Mum and I found it so surprising when Donovan's family unexpectedly turned up for an "intervention." They were demanding sounder, more compassionate care for their loved one and wondering what we did with our time. There were two of us managing this, after all. His dad, two sisters, one stepmother, and one brother-in-law came in for a cup of tea and some brutally honest truth telling. They were upset. Taking Donovan at his word, they demanded an end to the neglect and mistreatment. There were no solutions offered; they didn't want to chip in with the workload or share any care duties. They wanted their objections to be duly noted, and for the record, they loved Donovan so much, they would even have a confrontation on his behalf. Mum and I were positively shaken by the accusations and wanted to spend more time reeling from the audacity of it—not to mention the sheer size of their elephant balls—but we couldn't. Donovan was hungry and tired from the confrontation, there was a school project due, spelling words to memorize, and I still couldn't drive. The in-laws left and I got Donovan ready for a nap.

"I only wanted to vent. I didn't mean for them to come here like that."

"What did you think would happen when you told your family that you were being treated badly?"

"I don't think when I get upset. You know that. I do and say things that I don't mean. I am sorry."

Donovan's loss of control over everything that mattered was replaced with attempts at control over as many other things as he could . . .

"Drive in this lane."

"Poke the potato more times before baking it."

"Put this sock on first."

One of his assisted devices was a voice amplifier, a speaker that hung on the back of his chair attached to a headset microphone. It gave him the ability to bellow my name and be heard throughout the west side of town. (We thank you, Lord, for the delay in Bluetooth invention. For today, it surely would have been my demise.)

In one of my more stellar moments, I burst into tears at the sound of "HAAAAYYYY [breath] LEEEEEYYY" just as I lowered myself into a well-planned, long-overdue bath. I marched, towel wrapped and sudsy, to Donovan as he sat at his computer, and I turned the knob of his amplifier to the OFF position. I then threatened to wheel him to the bottom of the garden and leave him there in the rain. It was in these moments, the ones where I felt desperate, sad, and ashamed at my lack of patience, that I would call my mum. And if she were working, I would call Christine.

It was Christine I called at one of the worst times I can recall. It was a time when Donovan needed the bathroom (yes, another bathroom intervention, sorry). I sat him on the toilet, as per our usual practice, and left him in peace until he was finished. During that time, Dylan had a diaper explosion that needed my immediate attention. It was a race against time to minimize the damage of a fast-moving toddler with poop coming out the ankles of his trousers.

"I'm ready," came the call from the bathroom.

"Okay, give me a sec; there is a poomergency."

"I have to get off here. It's uncomfortable."

And I get it—not just in a way that you or I would be uncomfortable—but also in an inability-to-move or adjust-your-position uncomfortable.

"I know. I will be there as soon as I can."

"Haaaayyyleeeyyyy!!"

"You will have to give me a minute"—with a too-quiet-to-hear "for fuck sakes."

"Hayley, Hayley, Hayley . . ." he was screaming and repeating. I finished up with the baby and walked a few steps to the bathroom. The screaming continued; I wanted to be the yeller and tell him that I had to change the poop-spreading baby, but his upset was too great.

I switched gears and tried to soothe him. I told him I was sorry. I offered to move him and make him comfortable, but it was adding fuel to his fire. He was crying and the words no longer made sense. He began swinging his body sideward and banging his head against the wall. I put my hand there to cushion the blow and was shocked at the force he was creating. I shouted at him to stop and tried a restraining-type hug.

He bit the skin on my shoulder.

I stepped back and expected him to recognize that he had crossed the line, but the head-banging continued. I left the bathroom and returned a moment later with my bicycle helmet. I wrestled it onto his head and did up the chin clasp. Then I gathered up the children and walked them to the park.

That's right. I left my severely disabled, emotionally desperate, terminally ill husband sitting on the toilet. I called

Christine, told her what I had done, and she came right away. She shuffled her day, and dropped what she was doing. She didn't judge. She didn't say I'd done a terrible thing. She didn't tell me what she would have done or where I went wrong—she just helped. When I got home, Donovan was asleep and Christine was washing dishes. She wrapped her arms around me and said, "It's all right, my love—he's better now. And I told him that I would smack him right in the gob if he pulled that nonsense again." So assured my angel with the potty mouth and Cockney accent.

Along with Christine, there was another godsend at the exact right moment. My uncle and aunt came to Canada from Wales for the first time to stay with us, and we were reunited with a little bit of back home. This also meant *a driver* was in the house!

Hallelujah!

It was a bit past Christmas, but a miracle, nonetheless. Let me tell you, driving in a Canadian winter is a skill that many Canadians forget on an annual basis, so for a foreigner, it is much more difficult. However, my uncle was a rock-star driver. He stopped at *most* stop signs and successfully drove us everywhere. We escaped our confines and spread our wings to all of the fabulous touristy hot spots we could, and it was a glorious vacation for all of us.

As the end of their fortnight drew to a close, that familiar sting of sadness made an appearance. Except this time, it was a little different. It felt heavier and more sinister. The feeling of suddenly being placed in a wonderful situation with help, laughter, and shared camaraderie does not translate well when the situation is reversed. Knee-deep in the knowing that the exaggerated daily struggle was imminent was too much to bear. I tried to shake the dread of what was coming and enjoy the last moments of being with some of my favorite humans.

I almost succeeded.

For our last hurrah, we had a personal support worker come to watch the boys and Donovan. Mum, Aunt, Uncle, and I went out for the evening. Donovan wasn't feeling up for the event; he was tired from being sprung from house arrest, having enjoyed an outing during the day. His support worker would put him and the boys to bed and the rest of us had from 6:00 until 9:00 p.m. to eat, drink, and be merry. I was the drinker instead of the driver and I indulged.

We arrived home and I was giggly and probably a little wibbly. It would have been a perfect time to say goodnight, so I poured us all drinks. When it was time to admit defeat, we cleaned up some evidence and got ready to turn in. The house was quiet as I sat on the toilet in our tiny bathroom and contemplated the end of my respite just hours away. The quietness seemed to grow so loud in my head and I realized, as I sat there, that I was in way over my head. It was a physical pressure, a constriction and pounding in my neck and ears that was accompanied by screams of failure and fear.

You can't do this anymore! They need someone better, stronger, and more capable.

You fucking failure.

I could see clearly, and I could see nothing. It was like looking through a funnel; the vision and focus were on real things in my bathroom but seemed to narrow in my line of sight. So narrow that when I unwrapped the blade designed to fit into a callus remover, I couldn't see the whole of it. Unwrapping the seam was clear; but the edges blurred.

The pounding and screaming was an unbearable pressure; it had to stop. I sat on the bathroom floor, reached into the tub, and opened up my left wrist. The blood was dark—a stark contrast to the white of the bathtub as it made its way to the drain. I could hear the trickle as it fell downward into the drain. I could hear the trickle, not the crushing noise in my head. It was enough.

Relief.

"C'mon, missy, you've been in there for ages." Did I think everyone was in bed? When I didn't answer, my aunt opened the door and screamed. Mum and my uncle joined us in the tiny bathroom and moved quickly, doing the practical things required.

"What did you do? You stupid girl," Mum cried. Momentary relief of my silenced brain took a back seat to the guilt and disgrace I felt when I looked at the faces of the people I loved. At that moment, it felt like a mortal wound. Not my own, but one I had inflicted on the very people that held me up. The sudden remorse and profound shame that ensued were far worse than the wound.

The injury was patched, blood was wiped, and collective lies were told to hide the truth and keep the awful secret among the four of us. We never spoke of it again. I really have no understanding of how deeply I hurt them. I can only imagine that, like me, a lump rises in their throat along with a wave of sickness that washes over them until they wrestle that rogue thought down and tuck it away—way back in the vault. For me, that faint reminder wrapping itself around the inside of my wrist brings back the pain a little more often. When it makes an appearance, I hurry that thought back to its shameful corner—but not before I hate myself for the trauma I caused.

It was four months after the "poisoning" when I finally got my driver's license back. I drove Donovan to an appointment where he was assessed and prescribed an antidepressant, as well as a drug that complemented the antidepressant. Then, an antipsychotic medication and sedatives to manage his mood, anxiety, and behavior. These "helped" by making him absent and flat. The extreme behavior lessened, but so did the joy and personality. He did not accuse me of attempted murder again.

Of course, ALS caused none of this, because, according to medical science, the disease does not cause deterioration or alteration of the sufferer's brain.

CHAPTER 17

Scruff

I AM A DOG PERSON. That is all I can say about having a dog in a life that was mostly chaos. Also, I believe that all little boys should have a dog. If I had little girls, I would likely say the same.

Our Jack Russell terrier, Scruff, also known as Scruffy, Scruffers, and Scruff-scruffer-descruffscruff, was a reject, which made him an extra perfect choice. He was surrendered at four months old, along with many other short-falling dogs, to a shelter for JRTs failing to be like Eddie, on the '90s sitcom *Fraser*. He was a white, wire-haired Jack with a brown splodge over one eye. He was easygoing, loved the kids, and had a weird underwear fetish. His back leg did this hilarious sidekick when he was trotting along, and he didn't have a mean bone in his body—unless, of course, you were a raccoon, then look out! (Or, if you were something small and furry, I wouldn't take a chance. RIP, Doreen the hamster.)

On weekday afternoons, I would put my husband in his power recliner for a nap while I corralled the day care kids out for the school run. At this point, Donovan's balance was unreliable and his gait unsteady. There would be no unauthorized walking around. There had already been falls—spectacular and toddler-like in that Donovan was unable to put his hands out to save himself. A variety of minor injuries were patched up and laughed about later, but we were terrified of a serious fall, so standing or walking was a strictly supervised activity. Every day, Scruff would curl up on the chair and nap with Donovan as he was left in his "prison chair"—a safe spot where he wouldn't have to move until I came home.

Scruff was his protector.

In the warmer months, this could be as long as a couple of hours as the kids played at the park after school and ate goldfish crackers until home time. I dawdled home on one of these sunny afternoons, kids in tow, for a final baby bum change before pickups. I unlatched the gate to our deck, freeing the stampede of tiny feet. Before even opening the back door, I heard Donovan calling me. *Good God, man, let me take my shoes off!* I rushed to the living room to find Donovan—an unwilling participant—and Scruff, in an odd game of fetch. It was my husband's limp arm that was the object being fetched. Sometime after being left alone, Donovan's unruly arm fell from his lap and dangled limply over the side of the chair; he lacked the strength to correct this situation without help. Scruff to the rescue. Scruff leaned over and tried to retrieve the arm from above and pull it back up to its rightful spot. No luck. He jumped down and tried to leap back up with the arm in his mouth. Again, no luck. He repeated this pattern of attempts until I walked in to find a fully defeated Donovan and a panting dog, barking at a dangling, scratched and bleeding, very uncooperative arm. I picked up Donovan's lame arm and laid it across his chest. Scruff hopped back up onto Donovan's lap and assumed his position. Everything was right once more with the world; Scruff's little dog world, that is.

The wounds were superficial and hardly needed bandages. Donovan tried to lodge some sort of complaint, but I assured him that his sacrifice was a damn honor because Scruff was obviously, irrefutably, the best dog on the planet. He'd worn his little body right out trying to save that arm, out of sheer love.

Scruff frequently took it upon himself to give Donovan a good face wash. Usually, before a nap, Scruff would hop up onto Donovan's lap while he was in the power recliner. Then he'd stand on his chest to force him to endure a face licking. There would occasionally be nibbles; beards can be stubborn. Donovan didn't have the use of his hands so his objections could be verbal—with the inherent risk of being French-kissed—or he could turn his head from side to side and attempt to avoid the onslaught. Noting my husband's objections, I thought about intervening, but when I saw Scruff hold Donovan's flailing face still with a firmly placed paw on the left cheek, my heart melted. I know an expression of love when I see one. This was the only way to facilitate a decent eye cleaning. Awe, bless. This job was just too important to the hairy little bugger for me to interrupt.

He wanted the very best, cleanest human, so I let them work it out.

After all, dogs are people too.

Apart from a conservation area hike or a raccoon hunt, and the occasional self-directed escape walk around the block, Scruff's favorite thing was to be with my husband. (I thought about buying him a tag engraved with, "Fuck off! I'm not lost!") They slept together on the recliner every afternoon and on the hospital bed together every night. It might have been because my husband could dole out approximately zero discipline and Scruff did what he wanted—or it could have been the purest love known to man. Dogs are intuitive and just know shit.

Scruff had personality. He was a dick on a leash—he didn't just pull; he would back up then leap forward to gain even more ground. If you were in his company when putting on socks, he would grab the toe end and violently shake it until the foot-consuming sock had been defeated. My boys thought this was hilarious and never owned socks without holes. He was thoroughly overjoyed when absolutely anyone came to the door. He would always give a grateful chin lick before settling himself in someone's comfy lap. He was scared of manhole covers, and he once stole and ate a three-foot-long box of Christmas After Eight mints. Every bit of this changed when Donovan died.

Scruff joined us in being sad. He spent time in mopey solitude, and to be honest, I didn't notice immediately. His full bowl meant that someone had fed him, right? It took me a few beats to determine that he wasn't eating. He was encouraged to join his boys on the sofa—and by "encouragement" I mean Donovan-Rhys would reach into his doorless crate and carry him to the living room, forcing him into cuddles. He would escape as soon as he could. He stopped running to the door to greet people when they arrived. Scruff was entirely bereft; he also lost weight and started to pull out his fur. We gave him treats, love, attention, and people food. Nothing worked. When I took him to the vet, he had lost weight and needed a plastic cone around his head to stop him from biting the self-inflicted wounds on his raw skin. The cone did nothing to improve his mood. The vet prescribed topical medication, diet change, and suggested outrageously expensive tests and a consultation with a behavior specialist who might prescribe antidepressants. For perspective, this was at a time in my life wherein I had to go on a payment plan with the dentist because my son had a cavity. That bill took six months to pay off. The dog specialist was prohibitively expensive. Even if I could afford to see that doctor, it would have left me penniless and unable to buy the prescribed medication for Scruff, let alone food for my children.

On the second vet visit, Scruff had lost 25 percent of his body weight. I made the appointment out of desperation, but I didn't think that she could tell me anything new. She offered to rehydrate his limp body and I sobbed because my dog was dying of a broken heart. As we were leaving, the vet asked if I had thought about getting "a friend."

A dog friend?

"Might be worth a try," she said as I dripped snot over my sad pup.

On a farm-like property, in a dog hair–covered house about ten kilometers from home, a dog hair–covered lady was fostering several glum pups that had been rescued from a puppy mill. One of those dogs gave birth to a litter of puppies shortly after arriving in the new, safe home. On the drive over, I warned everyone that we were just *considering* this possibility, so, I maintained, "Don't get too excited." The jolly foster mum stopped arranging a kitchen counter full of dog dinners to show my sister, my boys, and me in. We worked our way through her kitchen to a baby-gated area that was probably once a dining room. In a roomy, comfy puppy box, a beautifully weary-eyed mama Jack Russell terrier watched over a litter of rowdy puppies. The foster mum released the barrier separating us from the puppies and all shoelaces were undone in about 3.2 seconds. My boys fell to the ground to experience the full puppy onslaught, complete with chewed earlobes and dismantled hoodie strings. We scooped up armfuls of pups and said things like, "You're so shmooshy," in syrupy baby-talk voices.

If dying of cuteness overload was a thing, I was close.

Yes, we came home with one—a baby girl. Dylan named her Olive after his favorite food: the black olives at East Side Mario's. She was a teensy, tiny Jack Russell terrier with black and tan splodges and a sweet, heart-shaped nose. We brought her into the room where Scruff slept and wallowed in depression. He didn't care that we had walked in, until he heard some unfamiliar whining—then he popped his head out of his crate. His ears pricked up for the first time in ages and he came to investigate this strange noise coming from my son's lap. For a terrifying second, it crossed my mind that tiny, furry creature Olive could be in danger. What if Scruff's prey drive kicked in and there was an actual murder? I had a brief vision of wrestling a puppy out of Scruff's clutches while he violently shook her with the kids screaming in the background. Before I could act on any of those possibly irrational thoughts, Donovan put Olive on the floor. Scruff charged toward her and she made a tiny leap to meet him, accompanied with a high-pitched squeaky bark. Scruff stopped in his tracks and lay down, paws stretched out in front of him, chin on the floor. He sniffed her a lot; copious amounts of sniffing, in fact. He bowled her over with his enthusiastic sniffing, and when he was done he sat and waited. Olive worked herself up onto his folded legs and fell asleep on him.

It was like flicking on a light switch. At that moment, Scruff stopped dying of a broken heart. He suddenly remembered that he was a hungry dog and his stubby tail wagged. He loved his new puppy friend, and they became instantly inseparable. He remembered that raccoons were the enemy and that underwear should be stolen and stashed in the back of his crate. He resumed the daily backyard perimeter check, joined us on the sofa, and fully came back into the fold. Who knows if he suddenly stopped grieving—or maybe he decided that some things were worth living for.

Or maybe, Olive caused just enough of a crack in his pain for some joy to seep through. It was as if he realized that Donovan's death was the end of that particular love but it was not the end of all love.

Scruff became a puppy again, wrestling and playing tug with Olive, and she learned to give in and accept being pinned down for a face wash.

Scruff was my faithful companion for seventeen years. He challenged me every day, and every day I reminded him that the humans were in charge. He greeted me with maximum joy on my best days and with the exact same enthusiasm on the days that I fucked up. He gave me the same consistent love and snuggles, without judgment, as I fumbled my way through raising two boys while looking after a terminally ill husband. And then as I fumbled my way through being a widowed single mum. He never complained about my cooking. He never cheated or lied, and that makes him better than most humans.

At seventeen and a half in people years, Scruff was mostly blind, mostly incontinent, and showed significant signs of dementia. The time came to stop being selfish and let him go. On his last day, my now grown-up sister came by with my brilliant, insightful six-year-old niece to say goodbye. This was our conversation:

"Aunty, how come Scruffy gets to die?" Kayley asked.

"Because, my love, he is very, very old and that has made him tired."

"How old?"

"Seventeen and a half."

"That is younger than you and Mommy."

"Right, yes, good point. But sadly, dogs don't live as long as people."

"Oh, yes. That is because dogs already learned to love everyone and be kind. People take much longer, so they have to live for more years to get it right. Bye, Scruffy." She two-handed ruffled his face fur and said, "Say hi to Tasha in heaven."

Who knows what awaits us in the next world? But for dogs, it could only be good things. If Scruff chose his heaven, he'd spend his days ridding the conservation area of raccoons then napping on Donovan's lap after a good face licking.

CHAPTER 18

Right Down the (Feeding) Tube

ASPIRATION PNEUMONIA is caused by foreign substances entering the lungs through the airway, instead of being swallowed. In Donovan's case, the muscles used to control swallowing were weak and he would frequently need to breathe mid-swallow, bringing on a coughing fit. The muscles used for coughing were also weak and they never fully cleared the debris. Since the lungs are simply not designed to have peas and carrots occupying them, the body would attack the intruders, causing inflammation and eventually infection. Donovan had several bouts of aspiration pneumonia.

He could no longer hold an eating utensil; and even if he could, he could not lift his hand to his mouth—so, he was fed. There were only a trusted few that could feed him properly. A small group he could rely on to master the food-to-fork ratio, the right timing, and recognize the moment the food should be switched out for the thickened water with a straw. Even with those specific skills, only five people could be trusted to make the experience a relaxed, comfortable, and natural one: myself; his dad; my mum; my sister, Kate; and my cousin Jonathan. At first, I thought that since my sister and Jonathan were young, they might not be able to feed a grown man—who was prone to choking—reliably and safely. But they were more than capable.

They were perfect.

I remember leaning against the doorframe, watching Jonathan feed Donovan and being in awe of the moment. Jonathan, in such an intimate moment of trust, fed the man he looked up to. The man who had taken him to a strip club on his nineteenth birthday. They talked and laughed between mouthfuls in a way that made dinnertime that enjoyable experience the rest of us take for granted.

The bond that these men had developed began in Jonathan's childhood on his visits to Canada from Wales, where he spent the summer underage drinking and getting frosted tips. Now it was a beautiful, extreme role reversal made possible by only the kindest and purest of hearts. How could someone as stubborn as Jonathan be so thoughtful and tender? My sister naturally fell into the role of caregiver; her empathy and love were masked in practicality and jokes because that can hide the pain. Nonetheless, her tenderness shone through in her actions. Never was this more evident than when I saw her turn Donovan's fork into an airplane and fly the food into his mouth. He almost choked because he was laughing so much.

During Donovan's second bout of aspiration pneumonia, he developed a deep vein thrombosis, or DVT. It is a potentially life-threatening blood clot that can occur with a lack of movement, like sitting on a long-haul flight. Donovan was unable to move when fighting pneumonia, and the DVT moved right in. He complained of pain in his calf, and when I touched it, it was hot. He was assessed and treated and ultimately released from the hospital with a treatment plan that included daily injections in the abdomen with blood-thinning medication. The prescribed medication came in multi-dose vials, which had to be drawn up into a syringe. The pharmacy provided a paper bag of needle-tipped syringes and instructions that advised on the dose of medication to be injected daily. There were also several alcohol-soaked swabs provided. It was thoughtful, but I was probably going to need a whole drink.

Donovan-Rhys and Dylan were fascinated and terrified. They watched as I drew up the medication and cleaned an area on their dad's belly, pretending to be confident while doing so. They held their breath and watched as I pushed the first injection I had ever given in my life into my husband.

They then erupted into shouts of, "Did it hurt, Dad?"

"Hardly felt anything," he assured them.

I asked the same thing when the kids were out of earshot. "Didn't hurt a bit, Nurse Hayley."

From then on, the boys were fully involved in medication time. It would be their first after-school job and they would take turns. They would clean the top of the vial with alcohol, match the dose to the mark on the syringe, then use a new alcohol swab to clean an unbruised space on Donovan's belly before giving their dad the injection. They would safely deposit the needle into the little yellow safety box and ask him each time to confirm that it still didn't hurt. The boys focused on the task at hand. They took it seriously and became confident and unafraid.

In the bigger picture, Donovan was getting worse. There would be more devices and equipment and procedures to scare the boys. Making them at ease with the changes around them was important. Being involved and trusted was important; feeling important was important. My trust in their abilities wasn't always aligned with Donovan's, probably because it wasn't my body being entrusted to them. Our boys thought it was a good idea to fart in the fridge then quickly close the door to trap the smell, so I understood the trepidation. We were doing our best to reduce the mystery and fear of procedures that could have been scary.

What the boys did not have to fear was what came next. Their thoughts stayed comfortably in the present, on their current task. My thoughts were not so contained. Donovan did have more pneumonia and a second DVT. Each condition required around-the-clock care, and with each recovery, a little more of Donovan was gone.

"You cannot afford to go through another bout of pneumonia. You definitely cannot afford another blood clot. I know you don't want to talk but I don't want you to die of something preventable. I want you to consider a G tube." Donovan had decided against invasive procedures to prolong life. This included being placed on a ventilator to breathe or having a gastrostomy tube placed for feeding. I disagreed with the latter. I forced this conversation as he was recovering from pneumonia, still suffering nausea and diarrhea from the harsh antibiotics.

"NO." It was labored but emphatic. "No tubes!" He was adamant. I cried as I challenged his decision and took advantage of his inability to argue back.

"When you are feeling better, you will be able to get in your chair and drive yourself around town. You will be able to take the boys for rides on your wheelchair and hear them laugh. You will be able to drive yourself to the arena and watch them play hockey, see them score, and watch them immediately look for you in the stands so they can see how proud you are. You won't just observe; you'll be able to participate in their lives." I was crying and he was still shaking his head. "Without it you are choosing to spend the rest of your life in a bed, dying of pneumonia, waiting for the next blood clot to break free and travel to your heart or brain. Or, maybe you'll be lucky and not get a clot. Maybe you'll just lose the ability to swallow at all, then you'll starve to death." I stormed out of the room. I was so right about this. It was a minor procedure that would make such a difference. It would make nutrition safe so he could enjoy his kids instead of always fighting secondary illnesses.

He conceded and agreed to at least have a consultation about tube placement. There was concern about his overall fragility and ability to bounce back from the procedure, but it was agreed that he would get a G tube. He had to be free of infection, finish his antibiotics, and stop blood thinners. It took a little while to get there, but the day finally came. During the procedure, Donovan was sedated. A long flexible wand with a light at one end was passed through his mouth down into his stomach. The light was used as a guide; when it was seen shining through the skin at the right place, an incision was made. The wand had the G tube port attached to the other end and was pulled through until the correct amount protruded and a valve was pulled against the stomach wall. Despite unstable blood pressure and vomiting post-procedure that required a great deal of suction, the tube was placed. Nutrition would be delivered through a gravity feeding tube directly into his stomach. There was some frustration as I learned the double clamp system before disconnecting, and there was some frustration as choking still happened. Kind of like tripping when you run up the stairs—no real explanation other than he would breathe in and take saliva in with the breath causing a cough reflex. He developed an infection at the tube site. A common occurrence, but the pain of it kept him fairly still while it healed. The pain of it was in addition to the other pain he was in regularly, which was substantial. He was given strong pain relief, which was delivered in a transdermal fentanyl patch. The dose increased to manage the new level of pain and it caused nausea, dizziness, and, when I could forget about my reality and be in the moment, some hilarious hallucinations.

"I don't want to get undressed in front of that dragon," Donovan once declared as I was getting him into bed. "Can you get rid of it?"

Perfectly reasonable request.

"Absolutely I can. No one gets to see you naked except me. And, of course, Christine, but that's not the point." I walked to the corner of the room and started ushering "the dragon" toward the door. "Come on, you. Out you go. Out, out, and stay out." I closed the door and turned to find Donovan slumped to one side, about to fall off the bed making a low groaning, gasping sound. I ran to him and wrestled him back up only to realize that the sound was laughter. He was having an uncontrollable laughing fit. I could do little more than join in with his contagious laugh while trying to keep him on the edge of the bed. It would be some time before he was able to regulate breathing enough to speak. When he finally did, I found out that he was laughing *at* me.

"It's still here," he managed to spit out before giving in to more laughter. As it turns out, I had missed the dragon entirely and escorted nothing out of the room. The dragon was still in its corner. Donovan found it hilarious that I was unable to see it. Unfortunately, not all hallucinations were funny; some were frustrating, and some were terrifying, but the reaction to them was equally emphatic.

The G tube solved some of the problems I anticipated it would. But it left others in their place. Donovan never fully regained the strength he had before his last bout of pneumonia and was never clearheaded enough to independently drive his wheelchair around town. Our boys had had their last ride with their dad, and we couldn't even remember whose turn it was. I had bullied my husband into getting the G tube. I pressured him and made him feel guilty for not making the effort to participate in any way he could with our boys. And, as it turns out, getting my way was the worst possible thing—and it was Donovan who paid the price. I stole his time, but more than that, I stole his quality of life. There were many times when I was not at my finest. I lost my temper; I became frustrated, desperate, and angry. At my worst, I yelled at my husband, kids, and plenty of others, leaving me with immediate regret and shame at my actions. This one was different. I stuck with it; I dug my heels right in. I felt right, triumphant, and good about leading the way for Donovan's new chapter. For this one, the regret snuck in quietly, growing day by day in increments equal to my husband's deterioration until it reached the size of shame.

By far the worst win I have ever experienced.

Not having a G tube placed would have had terrible consequences. Having the G tube placed had terrible consequences. I was left to guess which choice would have been right—or better—or given him more time on this planet. The weight of the choices we make for others is the heaviest. They don't become lighter with time; we simply become used to carrying them.

CHAPTER 19

Fight Like a Girl

"YOU'RE THE MAN OF THE HOUSE NOW." (Hair ruffle.) "You'll have to take care of your mother and brother." On the day of his dad's funeral, my son heard these statements from countless people. He was nine. When I heard the comments, I would intervene.

"Not quite," I would smile and say. "He's nine, so he will just focus on taking care of his hamster for now." I would direct him away, but I knew that the pressure was building. It wasn't said with malice or ill intent. It was worse than that, actually. It was said with no intent, no instruction or clarification. It was just what people said, without thought or commitment, blurting out the flawed, gold standard idioms of grief relieving.

There wasn't even a specific manly task he should start with. They could have asked, "Why don't you just [insert verb of choice here] like a man?" Problems can be more easily solved by being manly, can't they? The implication was that Donovan-Rhys should immediately give up childhood and be a man. Just do it. Stop being the lesser being of a child and assume the new, impossibly defined role you were given. By the way, your mother is also a lesser being of the female persuasion. She probably acts like a girl—or at best a woman—and will need taking care of. The point here is masculinity rules, and corrosive stereotypical opinions are nonsense. No, wait, that's not it. Bugger!

If only I didn't have a girl brain.

In the months to follow, those words stayed with him, and I couldn't eliminate their weight. As expected, this showed up in his behavior. The grief alone would have been enough for us to work through, but showing grief wasn't manly. How could he take care of us if he was sad? He began hiding his tears or angrily wiping at his face when he cried, all signs of weakness or an emotion that must be eradicated or hidden. He developed a scowl and a swagger and was defiant.

Not cool with me.

He challenged me, pushed his boundaries, and tested the limits. He didn't hold back when trying to stand his ground. On a day when the school called to report a behavior concern, it was time to draw a line. I had coddled him and let inappropriate behavior slide under the radar because I more particularly picked my battles after their dad died. So did the school.

"You are grounded, Donovan-Rhys—with no electronics." *There we go, a punishment.* That had been overdue for a while.

"This is bullshit!"

Um, I'm sorry, what? *What did he just say? Oh, good Christ.*
"The punishment stands." *That's it. Play it cool . . .*
"YOU CAN'T TELL ME WHAT TO DO!"

"Firstly, please lower your voice. I am two feet away from you with no hearing deficit. Secondly, yes, I can. It's happening right now. I am telling—" In that moment, my son stepped back into his bedroom and slammed the door in my face.

I want to say that I acknowledged his fragile emotional state and gave him the space and time he needed to breathe and calm down. But what I actually did was open the door, walk in, and engage.

"The punishment still stands. If you slam this door in anger again, I will remove it." I walked out leaving the door open. I was less than three feet away from the door when he opened it further to build momentum. He then used his whole body to slam it shut. I walked to the shed to find my power screwdriver. Then I searched the kitchen for batteries. As promised, the door was removed from its hinges.

"Dad would never take my door off!" This was now a long-distance shouting match through the house.

"No. He couldn't have done it himself. But had you behaved like this, he probably would have driven his wheelchair right through it."

"No, he wouldn't. He wasn't mean like you."

"That's right. I am Meany Mummy. Get used to it."

And then, for the knockout punch of the evening, hailing from the bedroom with no door, in the red corner . . . "I wish it were you that died."

Shall I box it up and gift wrap my heart—or will a paper bag do? I wanted to scream that I wished it were me too. Instead, with my wobbly chin and wobblier voice, I told him that I thought his anger was speaking for him and that if he still felt that way later in the evening, he could say it over again and I would give him the audience he needed to be heard.

The thing with my oldest baby boy was, he felt deeply. Seeing people with what he considered to be pain or sadness brought on the same in him. He once invited an elderly man who was eating alone at East Side Mario's to join us at our table. He did join; it was awkward, and then amazing. On Tuesday mornings, I took the day care children to McDonald's for a breakfast treat before the library opened. One day, Donovan-Rhys saw a person with a physical disability who was sitting alone, struggling to get into his McMuffin. He immediately left our group to sit with this person and help. On Fridays we rented a film from Blockbuster; Donovan would inevitably pick a documentary about saving sharks. (Dylan, on the other hand, always picked *George of the Jungle*. "Hey, watch out for that tree!" The Brendan Fraser version.)

We worked through his internal conflict about presenting his feelings as anger and having a stinking attitude. Car therapy worked well. I would put them both in the car and go for a long drive. It was perfect; the boys were actual restrained prisoners with nothing to do but converse. And that is what they did. Donovan's sadness crept upon him at night, and he would let it out. He would crawl into my bed, and then be able to sleep soundly. He did this for more than a year following his dad's death. I'd like to report that we talked our way into a healthy grieving process with no more attitudes requiring adjustment. However, it's important to note that the attitude and defiance were partly grief and partly the usual pre-teen crap followed by the Holy Grail: the teenage years. Fortunately, by that time, he knew everything about everything, so my worries were over.

Dylan's grief process was different and far more sinister. It began quietly, almost unnoticeably, in a predictable pattern of honest confessions of sadness soothed with hugs and snuggles. He then began displaying some spectacular tantrums, unreachable as he lost control over some benign trigger such as his brother absconding with the last chocolate Timbit or the hour of electronics time was over. From the behavior displayed, it was clear that the original trigger had little to do with the emotional breakdown. He pulled at his hair and skin. He punched the ground, hurt himself, and cried so hard it was gut-wrenching to witness. I watched him try to extract pain from his body until exhaustion forced him to submit. I could do nothing but attempt to soothe the tears that came after. His behavior was labeled as unmanageable at school, and he became a target for bullies. Given the nature of the outbursts, I asked that he always be supervised at school. I was informed that all children were always supervised. I furthered my point by requesting no solo bathroom breaks or solo time-outs.

Assurances were made. A few days following that request, Dylan arrived home from school, alone, in the middle of the day. He walked in the house after completing the twenty-minute walk, pulled a snack from his backpack, and sat on the sofa to eat it while watching *Blue's Clues*. He was seven.

He did not walk to or from school alone—he was always accompanied.

"Hi, Dyl. What's going on, pal? What are you doing at home?"

"In music, Brady played drumsticks on my head, so I played cymbals on his, then Mrs. Stamp sent me out to the hall for a time-out and that was not fair, so I came home."

I called the school and asked how Dylan was doing that day, and if there were any concerns. The secretary put me on hold while she checked with the teacher, she put me on another hold because the teacher was delayed getting to the phone, then asked if she could call me right back. The school principal called me ten minutes later to tell me that they couldn't quite locate Dylan.

"Do I have my facts correct? You're telling me that you have lost a child that you have labeled as having unpredictable and violent behavior?"

Principal Moron: "Not quite. The child isn't lost; he just hasn't been located yet. The custodian is searching the building."

Me: "When will you consider him lost, and what are the next steps? When was he, let's say, misplaced, and who misplaced him?"

Principal Moron: "I am working on answers to all of

those questions. I can tell you that if Dylan isn't found within the next little while, we will lock down the building and call the authorities."

Okay, enough.

"Mr. Moron, Dylan left school and walked home. It's a twenty-minute walk and he has been home for about twenty minutes. I asked that he not be left unsupervised. His teacher sent him to an unsupervised hallway and didn't notice when he disappeared."

There were obviously no satisfactory explanations that could be provided. I requested an educational assistant (EA) be assigned to Dylan and a meeting with the school board. Both of those things took time, and for the remainder of the term, my sister stepped up to watch the day care children while I went to school to supervise Dylan in the unstructured classes of music and gym. These were when the tantrums were most likely to happen. Not an ideal solution and an impossible one come September because both Dylan and I would be back in school.

During a car therapy drive, we passed through an impressive lightning storm.

Dylan: "Mum, if the car is struck by lightning, would we all die?"

Donovan: "No, because the tires are rubber, and we aren't touching anything metal so the electricity wouldn't reach us. Right, Mum?"

Me: "That's right; we are safe here in the car. It's pretty cool to watch though."

Dylan: "Aww, that's too bad. I thought we could all die

together and be with Dad. I thought about dying because I want to hug Dad, but I don't want to leave you and Donovan-Rhys. It would be great if we all died."

My family doctor referred us to a child psychiatrist.

After a summer reprieve where tantrums were just as fierce but less frequent, the return to school arrived with promise and mystery. In the hope of being a better provider for my boys, I went back to college. In hopes of a better term, Dylan returned to school. The new teacher was pleasantly surprised and thought Dylan was a joy. He was, until the bullying started. The torment was relentless and often led to frustrating Dylan-style meltdowns. He endured physical and emotional bullying from a small group of boys who loved to make derogatory dead dad comments. The school made a safety plan for Dylan's behavior, clearing the classroom so the children remained safe during an outburst. His tormentors often celebrated the victory of bringing him to that state and the bullies were not dealt with. My sister, who took over running the day care, was often called to go to the school. She would gather up the children to make the walk on almost a daily basis.

Dylan was at home more than at school.

On his first deliberate self-harm attempt, Dylan took a pair of scissors and superficially cut both his neck and wrist. Shortly following this, he tied his hoodie string around a doorknob to hang himself, leaving burn marks and bruising. The request for EA support was moved to urgent, as was the referral to the child psychiatrist. This last attempt followed an upset where Dylan brought his own basketball to school, which was taken from him by the usual suspects; he was then excluded from the game.

On my approximately six hundred and ninety-fourth trip to discuss bullying with Principal Moron, I was told, "Listen, I have done absolutely everything in my power to stop the bullying. At some point, you will have to accept that boys will be boys."

I'll go and pop the kettle on while you let that sink in.

Side note: I once walked into the office to pick up a misbehaving Dylan, and he and Mr. Moron were having a shouting match. Mr. Moron's face was red and there was a throbbing vein standing out on his forehead. I was honestly worried (OK, maybe hoping . . .) he might suffer a stroke.

Mr. Moron: "DYLAN. YOU ARE A DELINQUENT!"
Dylan: "OH YEAH? WELL, YOU'RE BALD!"
Me: "Hello. It appears that two people are having a tantrum here. I will take one away and that should ease some of the tension."

Dylan was placed with a shared EA and he loved her. She mitigated many potential disasters. He was seen by a psychiatrist who was small, soft-spoken, and whose very presence made us want to open up. She assessed Dyl on an ongoing basis and prescribed medication for his depression. While no one wants their eight-year-old to take antidepressants, the medication did eventually help bring him back to me. But not before something significant happened. Following a bullying event at school, Dylan ran away from his classroom, crying. When he reached the top of the second-story stairwell, he climbed the railing and stood on the small ledge, distraught and readying himself to release his grip. His EA tried to soothe him and coax him back to the safe side. Principal Moron showed up and demanded that Dylan "stop this nonsense immediately." This did not serve to reduce tension and Dylan's upset escalated. His EA lunged for him and grabbed his clothing. Another teacher helped as he tried to wriggle free of his sweater. They pulled him to safety, and I was called to pick him up.

After that day, he did not return.

The school called daily to register the absence and Mr. Moron called to tell me that it was my legal obligation to provide my child with an education and that he would be informing Child Protection Services. I repeated my request for a meeting with a school board member present. I repeated this request to the school board, and, given that I was making waves, a meeting was arranged. Until then I would continue to keep my boy safe at home in his aunt's day care. He was the biggest kid in that environment, the little ones liked to play with him, and his aunty spoiled him.

When Donovan died, I thought once the sadness subsided enough to function, there would space to breathe. To become emotionally available and stop battling for everything required. It didn't work out that way; I still had to fight. During the illness, I spent years fighting for what we needed—fighting off death and fighting and advocating for every penny and every piece of assistance along the way. Afterwards, I thought I could stop fighting. I wanted to slump in the corner of my ring and ice my bruises. Then my bank denied my mortgage life insurance claim and I had to fight. Ultimately, since the bank could afford excellent lawyers and I could afford none, they won. The decision was based on a medical finding. Donovan had been diagnosed with a trapped nerve in his shoulder before our mortgage application. The equation was complex, and math isn't my strength. Nerve = nervous system = (+/-) neurological (time) preexisting x neurological disorder = *Boom* (no money for you).

I fought with creditors for money Donovan had borrowed via online applications that I knew nothing about. He had even obtained a credit card in person at a pop-up —"*apply for a card and you'll get this piece of shit gym bag*"— stall, where the salesperson "helped" him sign. I fought with bill collectors, equipment collectors, my in-laws, and myself. Every fight came with its own set of worries. None as big as the worry for a boy who was ferociously tormented. So much so, he didn't want to stay on the planet with us. To him, death was a kinder option, and in those impulsive, desperately anguished moments, he tried to go there. It was soul-destroying. While going through something no child should have to, he went through a bunch more things that no child should have to. I wanted to follow him around the schoolyard screaming at kids, "Be fucking nice!" I wanted to punch his bully in his nasty eight-year-old face, stab his basketball, and threaten to burn his house down while he slept. Yes! I'm aware of my irrationality.

Back off.

On the meeting day, I tried to be as prepared as possible. A very smart friend attended with notes and points we had prepared, so I didn't miss anything. Dylan's psychiatrist came to present some damning evidence against the school. Dylan's classroom teacher, who was 100 percent in Dylan's corner; Principal Moron; a special needs education consultant; and two school board members were there to discuss the bullying, its effects on Dylan, and how to move forward. Mr. Moron started by explaining that he had done everything in his power to resolve the bullying, but Dylan insisted on making himself an easy target. I asked Mr. Moron to be precise in explaining his efforts; I wanted to know everything he had done. He did so and his short list of examples included reaching out to and meeting with the parents of the boys. I knew this not to be true. My sister knew one of the parents well, brought up the bullying, and had that difficult conversation. The parent was unaware and disturbed by the news. She punished her son by ending his beloved hockey season early; she hung his skates on the back of his bedroom door as a reminder. He was required to visit Dylan at home to apologize, and after the school board meeting, she requested that he be moved to a different class, away from the ringleader. This prompted me to contact the other parents; they, too, had not been contacted by Mr.

Moron and had no idea of their boys' behavior. Mr. Moron's failures and lack of integrity were made apparent. Dylan's soft-spoken psychiatrist then quietly offered her observations and findings. She gently used words like *borderline criminal*, *negligent*, and *dishonest*. She held the school board responsible and made mention of "reprehensible incompetence" for their choice of principal. She ruthlessly excoriated those responsible in the most soothing way. It was both terrifying and comforting to watch. This unassuming lady was one bad bitch. The school board representative asked what the desired outcome would be. I requested alternative education delivery in a small class setting with transportation. The educators and doctor agreed, and Dylan was enrolled in a small program for the three remaining years of his grade school education. There were twelve children and three staff in his class and he became engaged, focused, and happy.

I had become weary of fighting. I was so tired of pushing boulders uphill; I could have taken a nap on a clothesline. Still, though, I marched into battle with the school, the school board, and that dick of a principal. I assembled an army and a strategy, and headed into combat. This fight, this most important fight, I won.

My prize? My safe and happy son.

CHAPTER 20

Best-Laid Plans

DONOVAN DIDN'T WANT TO HAVE HIS LIFE supported with a ventilator; he wanted to stay at home with no further intervention. His lung capacity was diminished—he was unable to cough or clear secretions without the aid of suctioning, postural drainage, and position changes. It was time to make a plan, a *do not resuscitate*, or DNR, order that included advanced directives, so his voice was heard, and his wishes were followed. He talked with the occupational therapist who organized official papers; then with the family doctor who explained the process and prescribed sedatives should he panic when he became short of breath. Donovan was tired and weak; he had an alarm to let me know when he was in trouble and needed help or suctioning—or another intervention. He used that alarm many times a day. He used it the day after this solid end-of-life plan was fully understood and put into place. I took my hands out of the dishwater and dried them as I walked over to silence the alarm and clear his airway. This time the blockage was more severe—he was grey; his eyes were wide and panicked as he struggled to breathe. I called for my mum as I rolled him onto his side and grabbed the suction machine. This was the worst attack I had seen. If Mum was as scared as me, she didn't show it. She leaned him over and repositioned his heavy, uncooperative body to allow for drainage while pounding his back with the heel of her hand, all the while telling him, "Let's get this up; you'll be fine." It wouldn't budge, he wasn't moving enough air, his efforts were slowing, and cyanosis was creeping into his lips. I grabbed the phone from the base, put it on SPEAKER to call 911.

Shit. The plan.

The paramedics worked quickly, used their own suction machine, and provided supplemental oxygen through a mask that forcefully delivered it with every squeeze of the bag. Donovan was unconscious and the paramedics were breathing for him. They drove away using lights and sirens and I drove myself up. Damn it! I didn't stick with the plan.

In the Emergency Department, the doctor explained that Donovan was sedated and breathing independently with an oxygen mask. He had been admitted and was waiting to be moved to a ward. I could hear the effort of each congested breath over the sound of my own pounding heart. I thought he was going to die before I got there. Just as Donovan's dad arrived, the doctor asked if we could talk for a moment. He told us both that the situation was ominous, and that recovery was unlikely. Donovan had only very small areas available in his lungs for gas exchange—he estimated less than 10 percent—and he hung an X-ray of Donovan's chest that showed small dark areas at the top of each lung. I asked if those were the congested areas. They were not; those areas were the available space that was left for receiving air. My father-in-law pointed out that we already knew how dire the situation was—that was why we had a DNR and a plan in place.

Donovan was moved to a ward; his medications were adjusted, and he was comfortable. He mostly slept. When he did wake, I told him, "Sorry about the plan; I wasn't ready."

"Me either."

Relief.

He asked me to bring a notepad the next time I came to visit. We spent time writing letters that he slowly dictated to me filled with the thoughts he wanted to leave with the people he loved. It was a slow, heartbreaking process. I would often look up, waiting for the next sentence, to find him asleep.

His day shift nurse, Rachael, came in, carrying a stack of towels and a basin to announce it was bath time. She was young, bubbly, and knew her job well.

"My"—*breath*—"wife can"—*breath*—"do it," he protested in his raspy voice.

"Of course she can," Rachael replied. "She is awesome and already told me that if you guys had had a baby girl, she would have been named Rachael. The woman has great taste. She is also going to take the night off and go home and have a big glass of wine—and I am giving you a bath, my handsome friend."

I gathered my things and kissed Donovan's head. "Marching orders." I shrugged. "Can't argue with that. I love you. I will see you in the morning. Don't die, please." When I got to the door, I looked back at Rachael, blew her a kiss, and mouthed the words *thank you*. She winked in my direction and continued her task, asking Donovan if he would like the soap that would dry his skin so much it would resemble reptile scales—or the soap that smells like asphalt being poured?

Mum was home with the boys; they filled me in on all the important grade school news and then the three of them told me a collaborative whopper about how much homework got done and how much GameCube time there had been. The boys were fed, clean, and ready for school the next day. My amazing mum had everything organized, laundry done, and the floor vacuumed. She pointed out that it was surprising what can get done when there wasn't an alarm going off every five minutes. Then it occurred to me—holy shit; tonight, there wouldn't be an alarm going off every five minutes. "If there were any in the house, I'd have a glass of wine. Nurse's orders."

"That's why I brought this . . ." Mum pulled a bottle of white wine from the fridge. Once the boys were settled, we shared it, uninterrupted, while catching up on the day. Mum walked herself home and I sat in front of the TV, telling myself that I should use this time to sleep, but I was enjoying the alone time too much. Then I felt guilty for enjoying the alone time, so I called the hospital to check. Everything was fine. Don't call back. Enjoy the night off.

I had fallen asleep during *Prison Break* and was startled awake when the phone rang. It was the hospital; they needed me to come back as soon as possible. I was kicking myself; I had to call a taxi because I drank half a bottle of wine. I let Mum know that there was also a taxi on the way to pick her up, so she could stay with the boys. I took that same taxi that brought Mum to me to the hospital and asked the driver to please hurry; my husband might be dying. He asked if there had been an accident and I gave him a quick synopsis while noticing that I was wearing one of my running shoes and one of my mother's. We pulled up in the circular driveway of the hospital entrance and I thanked the driver. I offered the payment with one leg out the passenger door. He closed his hand over mine without taking the money. For the first time in our short encounter, I looked at my taxi driver, this kind, middle-aged man who had been listening to me, hearing me, while I was busy already forgetting this brief moment in time. I paused and took a breath; he gently pushed my hand with the money still in it back toward me and told me that he would be praying for my husband and me. I thanked him, this time because I was grateful.

The elevator ride to the third floor felt like it took approximately one week. The doors opened and I stepped out, into the same familiar, clean, wide hallway that was dimly lit for the nighttime. Light poured out of one room, illuminating a custodian cart parked on the opposite wall. Donovan was sitting up, leaning forward and struggling to breathe; there were nurses on either side supporting him, so he didn't tip one way or another. The doctor and on-call respiratory therapist were standing at the foot of the bed. The doctor was holding the chart containing a copy of the advanced directive outlining Donovan's wishes. I looked at Donovan's grey face and dry lips and asked him, "Do you want help?" He nodded his heavy head, yes. I turned to the doctor and asked him to intervene and do what he could. I expected orders shouted and a rush of activity; instead, the doctor calmly advised that if Donovan were to be intubated, he would, in all likelihood, never come off the ventilator.

Fuck.

What kind of choice was this? The respiratory therapist offered CPAP as a less invasive alternative that might help. All I knew was that it wasn't intubation, and it was doing something. *Yes. Please do something.* Donovan's face was placed into a mask with a wide, air-filled rubber seal around his nose and chin; it was held tightly in place with straps around his head. A loud machine forcefully delivered oxygen through a wide tube attached to the mask with every inhalation Donovan attempted. He needed coaching not to panic and let the device do its job; his nurse gently laid him back to a more relaxed sitting position while counting breaths with him. It was working. We bought some time, and once again, I failed to follow the plan. What was I supposed to do? Tell Donovan NO? Point to the paperwork and tell him that once the decision was made, there would be no going back?

"HELP ME!"

"Hmm, wish I could, but it's here in black and white."

"I want help. I don't want to die . . ."

"Should have thought about that before signing. Can I get you a sandwich instead?"

Donovan stabilized, the CPAP machine was replaced with a regular oxygen mask, and he tolerated it well. We finished our letter writing and I was heading to the airport to pick up my sister who was coming to Canada, this time to live here for good. The doctor asked to speak to me as I was making my way out about the next steps. He wanted to make an end-of-life plan. I said I would be taking Donovan home. He advised against it, telling me that the end is not always a peaceful process. I should spare myself the trauma and let the professionals take care of it.

I said I would be taking him home.

I returned later with my sister. I told her about Donovan's deterioration, his disorientation, and his altered state. I prepared her while we drove from the airport. When we walked into Donovan's room, he made me a total liar; he looked right at my sister, cracked the biggest smile, and said, "Kate!"

"Hiya, Donovan." She wrapped her arms around him.

"Do you know the muffin man?" Okay, there it was—the delusion brought on by lack of oxygen.

True to herself, Kate didn't miss a beat. She replied, "The one on Drury Lane? Yeah, sure, I know him." She took his confusion in stride. Donovan fell back to sleep smiling, clearly happy to see his little sister-in-law.

Nurse Rachael, on her fourth-day shift with Donovan, said that the confusion would most likely continue to increase as the oxygen saturation decreased; he would require supplemental oxygen at home. In his lucid moments, he was calm and ready to return home. Rachael got Donovan ready to go and helped transfer him to the stretcher that would be taking him back to our house. She made jokes about finally being able to eat a whole lunch or finish a shift on time now that he was going to be out of her hair. Between labored breaths, he thanked her for reading the news to him and for being a wonderful nurse.

He called her an angel.

We were approaching the elevator when I had to run back to his room to retrieve a small piece of sheepskin that was used to provide gentle padding between the bed and Donovan's heels. When I walked into the room, Rachael was leaning against the newly empty hospital bed, crying into her hands. She jumped and apologized when I surprised her, but honestly, I was the one who was more surprised. It hadn't occurred to me how affected she would be by Donovan's deterioration. How sending a patient home to die after making a connection was so much more than a job. For every patient she sent home, Rachael sent a piece of herself with them; she cried with them—and for them. She held her tongue, held her lunch, held her bladder, and sometimes just held them because she put the needs of her patients above her own. I was suddenly struck by how nurses find compassion through fatigue and make an impact few people acknowledge or understand.

"I'm sorry that you're sad, Rachael, but I am so glad that it was you. Thank you for getting us to this next part. I will never forget what you've done for us."

Before the transfer service brought Donovan home, we prepared the space. We met with the occupational therapist and family doctor to make sure that we were ready. Donovan was prescribed morphine for pain and sublingual Ativan for periods of anxiety. As a medical professional, administering narcotics and other controlled substances requires training, certification, and careful documentation. As the wife of a palliative man, it took picking up a brown bag from the pharmacy containing several boxes of morphine in glass vials, syringes, and screw-on needle tips.

Righto. I'll figure this out.

Our doctor explained that while the morphine was necessary to address pain and keep Donovan comfortable, it would also reduce his drive to breathe, as would the sedative. I asked her: Why, in all the thousands of years and millions of sufferings and dying people, was there not a more appropriate pharmaceutical choice? Why would the only medications that could bring relief also have the nasty side effect of hastening death? She assured me that, at this point, that side effect was not at all nasty.

Donovan was placed into the home version of his hospital bed, surrounded by medical equipment just like at the hospital. Except this version of a hospital had the sound of children playing, or occasionally fighting, in the background. We were home and now we would endeavor to follow the plan. It was time to wait, smile for my children, care for my husband, and hope for a good death.

CHAPTER 21
The First of Everything

THE FIRST OF OUR FIRSTS was completely unexpected and therefore considerably underestimated. My sister and I walked to the Cenotaph on a chilly November 11, to honor our veterans with hundreds of others at our town's Remembrance Day service. At some point during the moment of silence as the Lancaster flew overhead, I found myself trying to suppress snorting-type sobs. Kate nudged at me with a remarkably inadequate tissue, and as I glanced over, she was trying—but failing—to hide an ugly cry. As the crowd dispersed, we scarpered without looking up; one of us hanging onto the coat sleeve of the other until we were far enough away to breathe. When we were at a safe distance, Kate wondered, "What the fuck just happened?"

"It's gotta be allergies," I answered.

The actual first of our dreaded year of firsts was Donovan's fortieth birthday. Its approach was like volcanic lava slowly rolling down a mountain toward our house. The speed of its descent upon us remained consistent; the intensity of my fear of it grew exponentially with each burning inch it gained. The heat rose, igniting anxiety and anger that not even my reliable stream of tears could douse. Would this day render me broken and unable to function? Would I cry in public? Would I lie in my house and let the flames consume me? Given that we lived in a rather un-volcanic Canadian town, I doubted that my house would be engulfed in molten lava, although there were days I thought that volcanic pain might be more tolerable than my current heartache.

For the last few years before my husband died, as all the important dates rolled over on the calendar, I never knew if that particular day would be the last that my husband and I would share. Each occasion was celebrated as usual, instead of extra-special, last-ever-occurring occasions.

If only I'd known . . .

It was clear that the approaching day was both unstoppable and overwhelming. The only thing to do was prepare. Donovan's birthday would be celebrated with a party. I would like to tell you a whopper here and say I was fully on board; that I was in that party mood. That I just couldn't wait to put on makeup, cook a batch of premade sausage rolls, and fill the center of the plastic chip 'n' dip sombrero plate with medium-heat salsa.

I was not.

What I really wanted to do was curl up and let the day wash over me with a few tears, snuggles with my boys—who would remain blissfully unaware of the date—and maybe indulge in a self-destructive, yet cathartic viewing of *The Notebook*. The family—yes, all of them—had another idea entirely.

Donovan, along with his family and friends, were robbed of his fortieth birthday celebration. It came just weeks after his death—too painfully close for anyone to let slip by. And those people? They were hurting. They needed to participate. Their pain could only be measured by how much they showed up to hang banners, cook party food, share stories, and hug out the tears. My sadness was allowed to be immense; it was expected. Theirs was hidden under work clothes, deadlines, and all of the other continuations of life that demanded that feelings be halted for a more convenient time. This was not my day, not my pain, not my sadness, and not mine to keep hidden.

At this point, you have likely come to the conclusion that I am not a fan of grieving in a way that only comforts others. What I am a fan of is comforting others. Making that day invisible would only leave a void for the people who loved him, where there was a clear opportunity for comfort. My other wish was that we would keep Donovan present and talk about him every day in regular conversation, so his name would never be avoided for fear of causing distress. By hiding away, I would have been reinforcing the idea that Donovan was a subject too big for the room. I had to decide between what I wanted for myself in the saddest moment and what I wanted for all of us. My heart was too broken for the two to align.

I was already teary in anticipation of the faces I would be seeing at the party when it was still hours away. My sister thoughtfully made a sign for me to wear that read, DON'T HUG ME! I'M FINE.

She took it off me at the last minute, saying it was a joke. Rude. But she kept an eagle eye on me, making sure I wasn't overwhelmed. Later in the evening, she had to close one eye to see straight but still kept that wonky gaze my way. Familiar faces popped in throughout the evening with hugs and tears to share. It was emotionally exhausting but wonderful and affirming. Yes, after Donovan died, everyone went back to living their regular, busy lives. And yes, I was a little pissed about it. But they never stopped loving him. Part of each of them was a little bit changed for having lost him from their lives. My boys got to see how loved and missed their dad was—how he impacted everyone's world and how far his reach was. It was a hard thing—but definitely a good thing.

The next first wasn't a recurring calendar event but the first time I would be seeing Donovan's extended family since his funeral. It was his grandmother's funeral. The upside was that I had a funeral outfit to wear. The other positive—my sister would come with me so I wouldn't have to go alone (honestly, though, where would I be without her?). The downside: I was pretty sure that I was not emotionally strong enough to have a conversation with any of those people without breaking down. The service was at a funeral home. We parked and waited for as long as we could, leaving no time for chatter or meet and greet. Kate and I quietly slid into a row of plastic chairs, avoiding all but a couple of hello waves. Kate then reached into a shared colored glass candy dish with multicolored hard sweets. As she popped one in her mouth, I leaned toward her as we were all asked to stand and whispered that the dead person's hair and makeup artist probably put those out—and she *spit it back into the bowl*! The dull, pastel candies were now graced with one wet and shiny jewel.

After the candy incident, I began biting my lip so I didn't look like the idiot grinning at a funeral, but it was about to get much worse. As it happened, Donovan's grandmother died on her birthday. To acknowledge this, the small congregation was asked to stand and sing "Happy Birthday." Yes, the "Happy Birthday to You" song. Kate and I looked at each other to silently note our shared confusion and the utter absurdity of the request. Then we glanced around the room to take cues from the others. All of them looked equally dumbfounded, but no one was brave enough to object at a funeral. This had to be a joke and I wasn't going to be the first to fall for it. Nope, no joke. We stood up at a funeral and sang "Happy Birthday" to a dead person. This was a test of my steadfastness, and I was hoping that the results would be bell-curved. I had bent over to pick up a tissue that I hadn't really dropped so I could be out of sight for a second. While I was down there, my sister deliberately kneed me and I stumbled loudly into the row in front. I pinched her leg before standing back up.

We had to get a grip here; I couldn't be the widow who got thrown out of a funeral for being rowdy.

We managed to refrain from further trouble for the rest of the service and tried to make a run for the exit. We made sure to offer a quick smile and a wave to anyone we were forced to make eye contact with. The double exit doors were so close when Donovan's aunt stepped in front of us. There was no escape. She was actually my favorite aunt of his and was no stranger to hardship, which made it both better and worse. Better because she was someone I wanted to see (just not at that moment) and worse because she was genuine and lovely and said, "How are you, kid?" in her thick Northern England accent.

I was already crying. We shared a hug and said words while I tried not to have a full-on sob. I explained that I had to run. She must have seen my panic rise when I looked over my shoulder at the people emptying from the room. She nodded her head and I headed for the door.

In the car park, Kate turned and looked at my red and blotchy face and said, "Oh, for God's sake." She then bolted for the car, got in, and locked the doors. Honestly, nothing depicts love like being locked out of your own car while having an emotional breakdown. People, lots of people, were on their way out and they were all going to ask how I was doing. I kept glancing over my shoulder and pulling at the handle while shouting, "Oh my God, let me in!" I felt like the girl in the slasher movie that keeps dropping her car keys.

"Not until you've stopped that bloody sniveling."

"It's my car!" Kate looked at me with a face that indicated her profound disgust at the weakest argument I could have presented.

"C'mon now, I have snot dripping off my chin and people are coming."

She cracked the driver's-side window and leaned over. "Here. You can have this but that's it until you put your tears away." I reached for the offering.

"This is a recipe. I can't blow my nose in a recipe." I was truly hoping that she was in pain from laughing. I heard the door locks click, but each time I pulled on the handle, she'd locked them again, bringing about a renewed wave of that soundless laughter that happens when something is so funny that you're stuck, doubled over, mouth wide open until you can finally gasp a breath. I give her the death stare and she unlocked the door right as the horde of zombies broke free of the funeral home confines and stampeded my way. I started the car and we narrowly escaped the annihilation.

No thanks to my sister, who laughed until she cried.

There was never any real danger of our brains being eaten, of course. Those zombies were people who wanted to know how I was doing and let us know that they were thinking about us. But I couldn't face it because of anxiety. I didn't know it at the time. It didn't have a word or a label for the fear I had about becoming overcome with emotion. The fear of no control when I thought I should have, and needed to have, control. The fear of being judged and the need to flee. That liar, anxiety. It hides in the brain and whispers untruths, planting those seeds of doubt that we nourish until we question our own worth. It is so allied to grief that it should be added as a subcategory to each of the stages.

1) Shock and denial—and anxiety
2) Pain and guilt—and anxiety
3) Anger and bargaining—and anxiety
4) Depression—and anxiety
5) The upward turn—with anxiety
6) Reconstruction and working through—with anxiety
7) Acceptance and hope—and anxiety

On the way home, Kate and I stopped at our favorite diner for scrambled eggs. We both laughed at the bizarre circumstances of the service, and my sister continued to laugh at her own warped and excessively cruel sense of humor. When we were finished, I went to pull the car up while she ran to the loo. She came out and went to the passenger-side door, reached for the handle, and I pulled ahead.

"Yes, yes, I asked for that one," she acknowledged and reached for the handle. I pulled ahead.

"C'mon now," she pleaded so I rolled down the window and said, "Fine, you've learned your lesson. Get in." She reached for the handle, and I pulled ahead. I did it at least another ten times.

AMATEUR WIDOW

I'm sure everyone's year of firsts looks different. For us, Christmas came next, followed by Donovan-Rhys's and Dylan's birthdays, Mother's Day, and then Father's Day—which was particularly rough. My birthday and our anniversary were followed by the final one: the Deathiversary.

If you have gone through the year of firsts or are still going through it, you will get to the Deathiversary. There are some things that I need you to know about this milestone.

Firstly, you are a fucking warrior. You were 100 percent successful in surviving three hundred and sixty-five days of emotions that were often so intense, you doubted their survivability. Go ahead and be a pool noodle. For the times you kept it together, bit your lip, swallowed that lump in your throat, restrained yourself from punching someone in the throat, pushed your needs, emotions, tears, and frustrations way down in the deep, dark sadness of self-control—let go and let them burst through the surface. Release them into the sunlight and then let them explode into the world. Finally, be a pool noodle.

Secondly, express your needs. People love you, but if we know anything about grief, it is that we have no idea how to talk about it or act around it. No one knows what to say or what to do, and the result is often clumsy or hurtful—or, at best, inadequate. To the people who matter, say it out loud and be specific. Tell them that the date is coming, and you will need a text acknowledging it first thing in the morning, no later than 9:00 a.m. Tell them that you'll need all plans canceled and comfort food brought to you in the form of homemade mac and cheese with a nice bottle of chardonnay. Tell them to pick up party poppers and cone hats from the dollar store. Tell them to leave you alone. Whatever it is you need, tell them. They won't know unless you do.

Thirdly, don't "at least" yourself and don't let anyone else "at least" you. For example: "Well, my husband died but *at least* my entire family didn't die in the Rwandan genocide." My husband died—that was my ten. The worst thing that you have been through is your ten. Ten is ten. Your grief is worthy of being felt, no matter what anyone else has gone through. Comparing your loss to mine or someone else's has no value and certainly doesn't diminish your loss or tragedy. It simply makes you question your response to it. Put down the imaginary "how big is your loss" tape measure and permit yourself to grieve because loss is really fucking hard, and you have experienced it and earned every painful tear. "At least" is not a loss minimizer; it is a dismissal of the most intense feelings you have ever experienced. To compare our losses to one another is a hurtful competition where there is no winner. We have already lost too much.

So, instead of comparing what you've been through, know that I see you. I see your pain, your sadness and triumph, no matter your loss. I see your smile and what it hides. I see you on the days you can't face the world—and the days when finding matching socks is the only successful moment. I see you when you're too sad to go down the cereal aisle. I see you when you put on makeup and almost recognize yourself. I see you when you cry because you begin to reminisce when a song comes on the PA system at the mall.

I know about the lies you hear in your head because I've heard them too. What you might not know yet, what you may not have recognized, is your superpower. It is a secret that only those who have experienced loss can know, so keep it under your hat. As everyone else goes about their daily living between comfortable, well-defined margins, we, the grieving, have broken ours. We are no longer bound by those comfortable restraints that keep emotions manageable and safe within acceptable, normal standards. For us, those chains were broken when we were destroyed by sorrow.

For a while, we lived well below the emotional poverty line. And we will most definitely go back to visit again. But when we return, it will not be to the normal range of emotion. On the days we can, and there will be more and more of them, we will smile bigger, walk taller, and love harder. We will embrace the joy because we understand what life is without it. We will no longer safely be restrained, because we have earned a higher emotional pay bracket. And we are worthy. Our grief is big and it's okay not to be okay and it's okay to be stronger and happier than before. We did it. We made it all the way here.

We are magnificent fucking pool noodles.

CHAPTER 22

Fuck the Toronto Maple Leafs

OCTOBER 5, 2005, marked the end of a ten-month, National Hockey League labor dispute and lockout. The entire previous 2004–2005 season had been canceled, creating quite the drought for distraught hockey fans. Hockey, specifically the Toronto Maple Leafs, was Donovan's one true love. The team logo was tattooed on his arm.

A few years earlier, Donovan's good friend Barry walked into our kitchen and asked Donovan what he was up to that evening. He said that he was going to change it up by being fed his dinner on the sofa instead of his regular chair. When Barry presented Donovan with a pair of platinum Leafs tickets, it wouldn't have mattered if we were renewing our vows that night and the pope was in town to perform the ceremony. Seeing the Leafs play in their hometown while sitting in platinum seats trumped anything that could have been previously planned. Wheelchair access also meant that the seats were located in the best seating area of the platinum section. Donovan wept and tried to find the words to express his gratitude to Barry. This would be hard for most but was particularly challenging for Donovan, whose speech was failing, so he mostly made snorty noises. As if the evening weren't already unforgettable, there was an added surprise. The Toronto dressing room exited at the platinum seating area. The players had to leave their dressing room and walk through the platinum section to get to the ice. Seeing the idols of his team was spectacular for Donovan. But he didn't expect to see his all-time favorite Leafs player, retired icon and supporting alumni Wendel Clark, follow them out and then take a seat to watch the game. Wendel Clark and Donovan were only a couple of seats away from each other and Donovan was speechless; frozen in a sort of childlike, starstruck awe. During a break in the play, Barry asked Mr. Clark if he wouldn't mind taking a moment to say hello. Mr. Clark did far more than that. Donovan not only met his hockey idol, but Wendel also took the time to speak with his biggest fan, shake his hand, and have a conversation. Donovan couldn't lift his hand to reciprocate the handshake but Wendel didn't miss a beat; he picked up Donovan's hand and gave a firm shake as if it were the most normal introduction ever. Wendel Clark got up and left his seat during the second intermission. At the start of the third period, he returned with a beer, a hot dog, and a signed number 17 Wendel Clark hockey jersey. He told Donovan that there was no way he would part with his beer or his hot dog—but he could have "this old jersey." Donovan was ecstatic. Honestly, the Make-A-Wish Foundation couldn't have done a better job.

The announcement that the lockout was over was a big deal for Donovan. It was for all NHL fans, but for Donovan it was different. By this time, ALS had rendered Donovan mostly confined to his hospital bed, unable to move without the help of a mechanical lift and many hands. He was on oxygen, and being administered narcotics for pain. His breathing became extremely labored. I had decided to bring my husband home from his latest hospital stay. I brought him home to die and time was running out. Donovan didn't ever expect to see the Toronto Maple Leafs play again.

This was a huge deal.

For the first time in NHL history, all thirty teams were playing at the same time on that one night. Toronto would face Ottawa and continue a long-standing rivalry, and we would throw a hockey night party. Close friends filed in and crowded around Donovan's hospital bed to watch the game. Donovan slipped in and out of sleep, but when the *Hockey Night in Canada* theme song played, signaling the start of the game, his eyes opened wide and a smile crept across his grey face. Hosts Don Cherry and Ron Maclean returned to him like old friends, their banter familiar and back in its rightful place. Donovan worked hard to stay present—he couldn't speak at all well, but he tried. He definitely said "CHEERS" when friends would use a spoon to share a tiny sip of their beer, dropping a splash onto his lips just so he could have a taste. Our friend Dave, who had been there for so much of what Donovan went through, stood in front of the TV as the puck dropped. Donovan's eyes widened, and Dave, in his broad Cockney accent, said, "Tell me to fucking move." Donovan grinned at him. "C'mon then, tell me to fucking move." Dave moved in close to hear Donovan.

"I"—*breath*—"fucking"—*breath*—"love you." Dave grabbed his friend and pulled him close as he cried into his hair and pretended to punch him in the head. I ducked around the corner to dab at my eyes for the twentieth time that evening.

Combined with the sadness was laughter, along with the excitement of watching the game. Everyone there, at some point in the evening, sat on the edge of Donovan's bed and opened a conversation with something like, "Hey, buddy, remember that time . . ." Donovan nodded and smiled and worked hard to shift his hand onto his theirs, telling them with touch what he couldn't say with words. His family took turns being next to him, adjusting a pillow, massaging a hand, and whispering that they loved him. If there was one thing he knew more than anything, it was that he was loved.

At the end of the first period, our beautiful friend and neighbor Sue took Donovan-Rhys and Dylan home to her house. She no-nonsensed the boys' dawdling and reminded them to get a wiggle on because it was a school night.

"Give your dad a hug and tell him you'll see him tomorrow." They did, and Sue did the same. She used her thumb to wipe up the tear that bounced from her eye and landed on Donovan's arm. He held her gaze and they exchanged a lifetime of conversations without words before she squeezed his hands and left the house with his boys. At that moment, for one singular time, fatigue was his ally, softening the blow of watching his boys walk away. I stepped out into the cold evening air and breathed deeply. I counted my footsteps on the crunching gravel drive until the wave of panic/sadness/desperation passed and the urge to chase after my boys was under control.

Everyone who came that night hugged Donovan and told him that they loved him and that they would see him soon. Each person found it difficult to take the step out of the house that ended the evening for them. I could see it in their faces; the indescribable need to stop time, to change what could not be changed to make that moment less painful. When the game was over, my mother spent her time with Donovan before walking herself home. My sister, Jonathan, and I sat with a mostly sleeping Donovan to commiserate the Leafs' loss to Ottawa. They helped turn him, make him comfortable, and give him medication. Jonathan took a warm cloth and wiped the face of the man who had taught him how to punch and, much to my horror, took him to a strip club for his nineteenth birthday.

When Kate and Jonathan went to bed, I squeezed in next to Donovan and asked if he had enjoyed the evening. He whispered, between labored breaths, "Fuck the Leafs." My shoulders started to bounce, Donovan made a low moan sound that was a substitute laugh, and pretty soon I had to sit myself up to catch a breath and wipe away the ridiculous amount of snot and tears the crying and laughing had created. For a moment, he was so very awake, seemingly so aware. He had a big smile on his face, and it was my turn for the wordless conversation. Except he drew in as much breath as he could and tried to say all of the things. His mouth wouldn't cooperate, and he became shorter and shorter of breath. I held a finger to his lips and told him that the best use of his breath was not to waste it on me. I told him that I loved him, probably for the millionth time that day, desperately trying to make up for the days I missed. I racked my brain for the inspirational thing I was supposed to say next, the most important words that could not be left unsaid. Words failed me so I cradled his head against me; all that could be heard was his labored, congested breathing. His body relaxed and softened into the bed and his eyes closed. I settled alongside him in the narrow hospital bed, just for a few minutes, until he was asleep. When sleep took hold, I would pull my hip free of the hard, cold side rails and head to the futon. Until then, we were lying in the quiet, waiting for sleep, when he nudged me. I looked up to see his eyes wide open. As clear as any words ever spoken, Donovan said, "Be happy, my love." I promised that I would try. Donovan closed his eyes for the last time.

ABOUT THE AUTHOR

Hayley Redman has been a caregiver, day care provider, server, photographer, and is currently a paramedic. She has jumped from a plane, ridden a tuk-tuk in India, raised boys, and survived grief. Originally from Wales, UK, she and her husband now share their home in northern Ontario with two* extraordinarily adorable dogs and a flock of chickens. She is the author of the debut memoir *Amateur Widow*, which was on the *New York Times* Best Sellers List** for sixteen weeks. When she is not working as a full-time paramedic or writing books, Hayley loves to read, kayak, and repeatedly ask her husband if they can get another dog.***

---

* Now three.
** Not the *real NYT* best seller list. The made-up one.
*** It worked.

ACCOLADES AND PRAISE FOR
AMATEUR WIDOW . . .

"Less swearing than I thought there would be."
—Hayley's husband, Todd

"Wow, I really didn't need to know about my daughter-in-law's sex life."
—Hayley's mother-in-law, Linda

"Thank you. You put words to how I feel. Your book has given me hope."
—A lady who recently lost her husband

www.ingramcontent.com/pod-product-compliance
Lightning Source LLC
Chambersburg PA
CBHW031106080526
44587CB00011B/843